K. Rose's
Covers and Characters
Coloring Book
2023

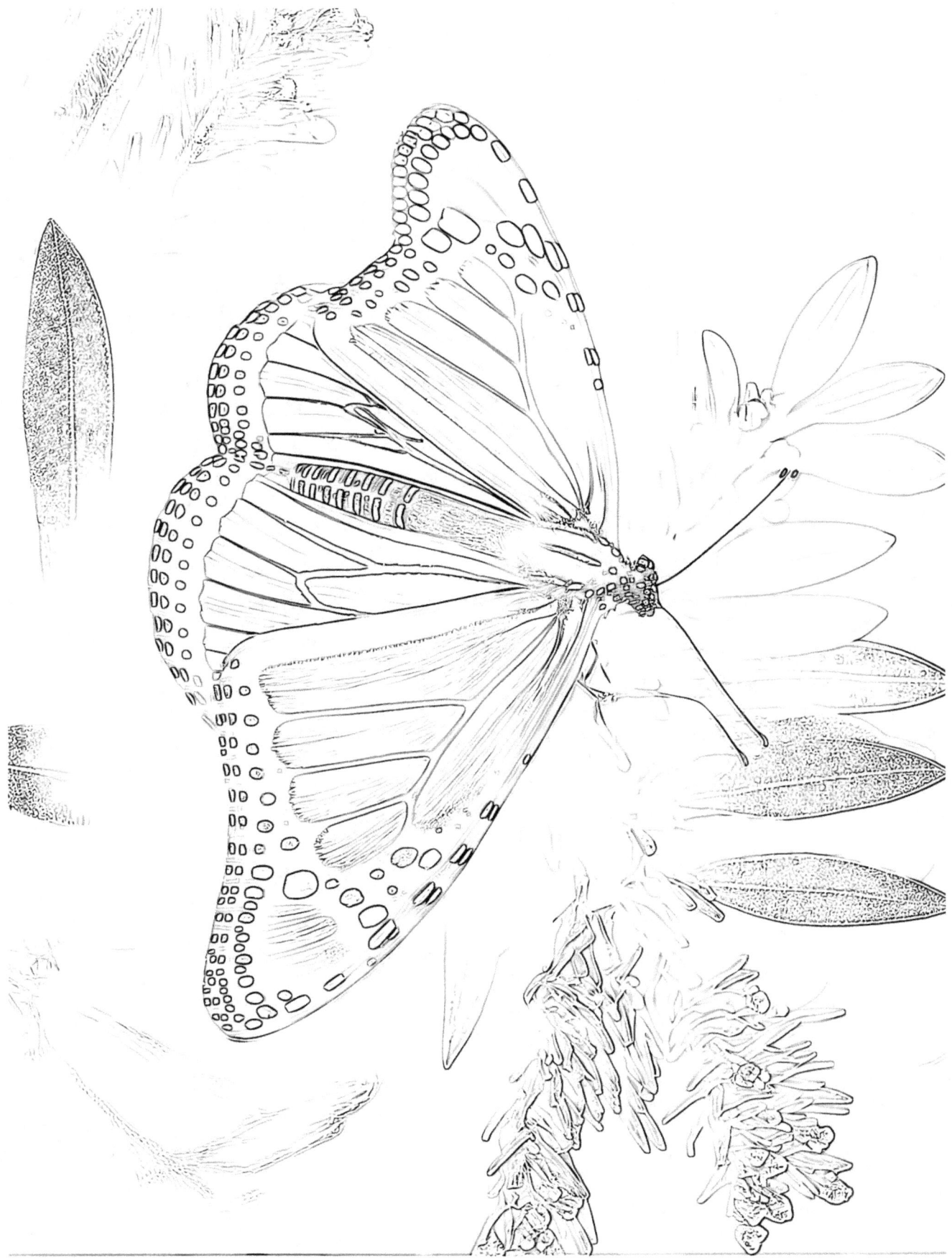

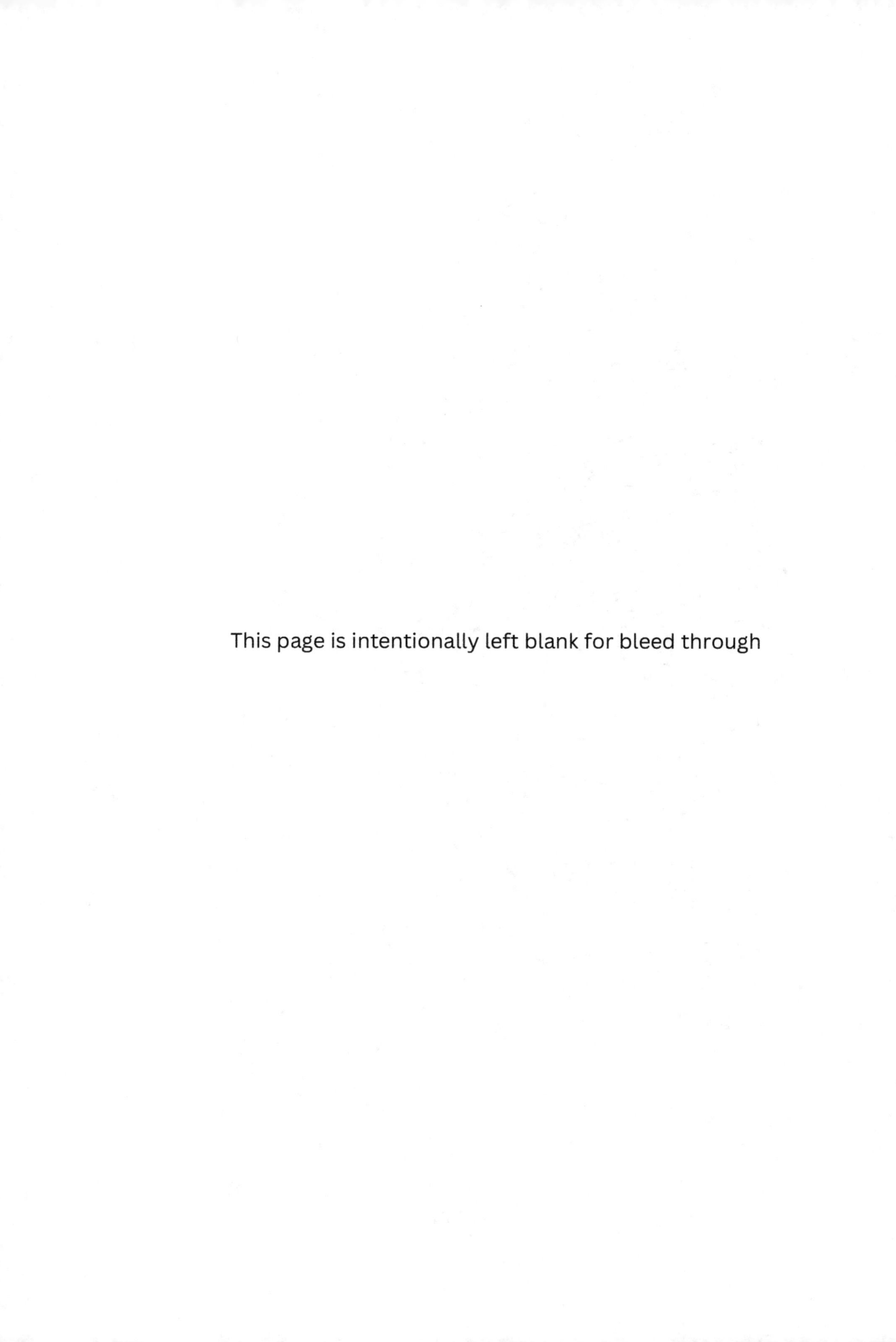

This page is intentionally left blank for bleed through

The Flying Huntress

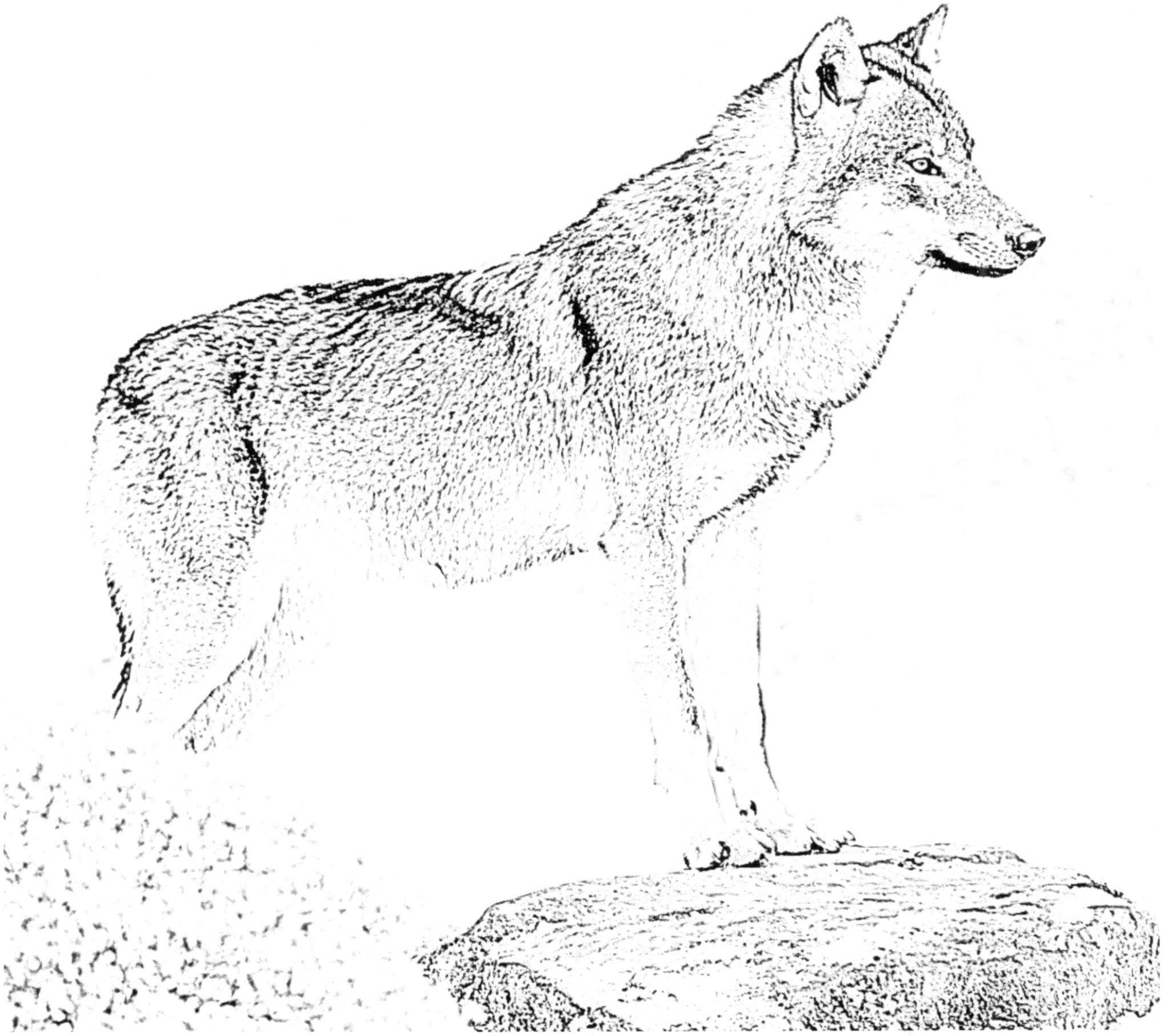

This page is intentionally left blank for bleed through

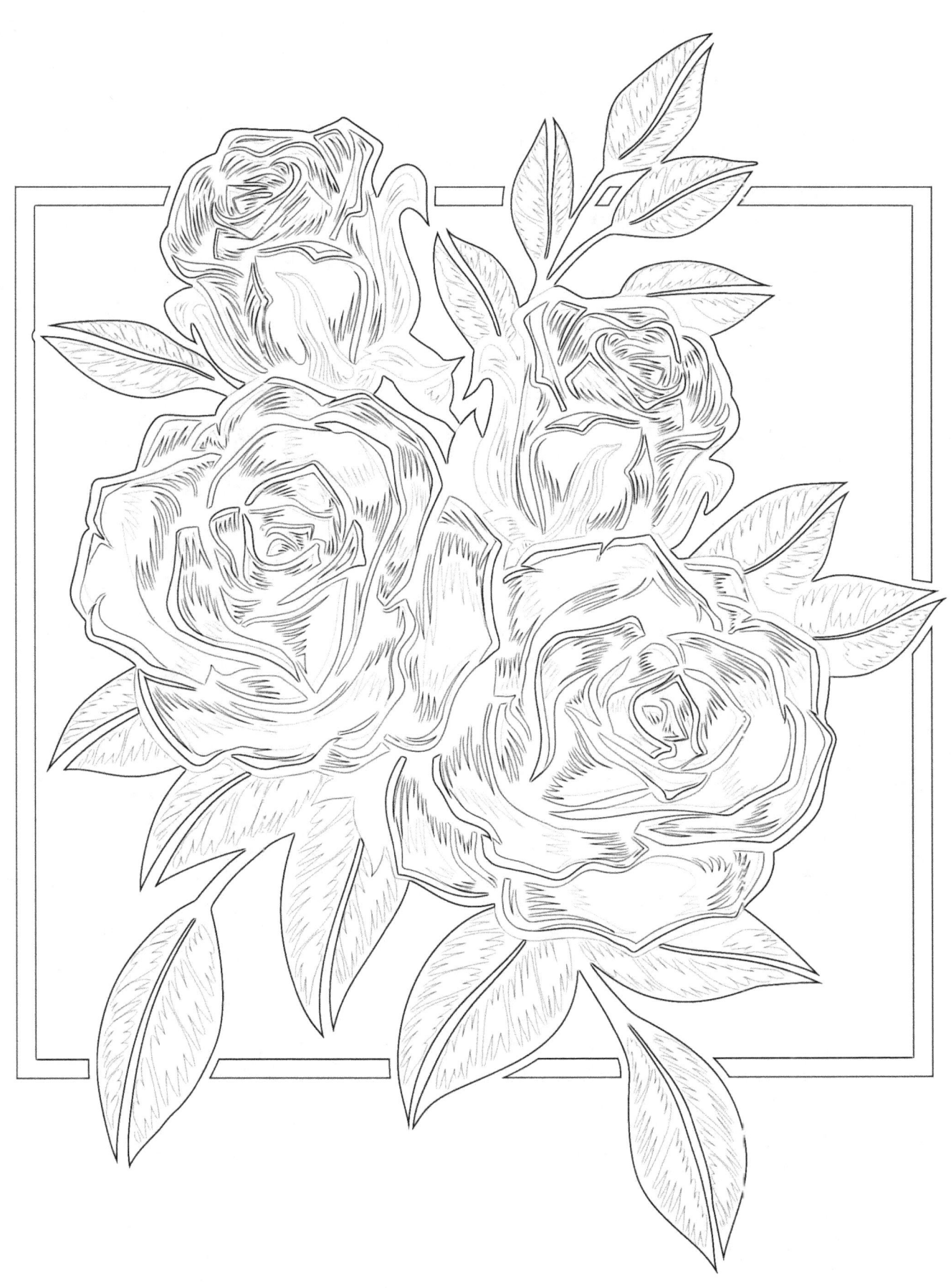

This page is intentionally left blank for bleed through

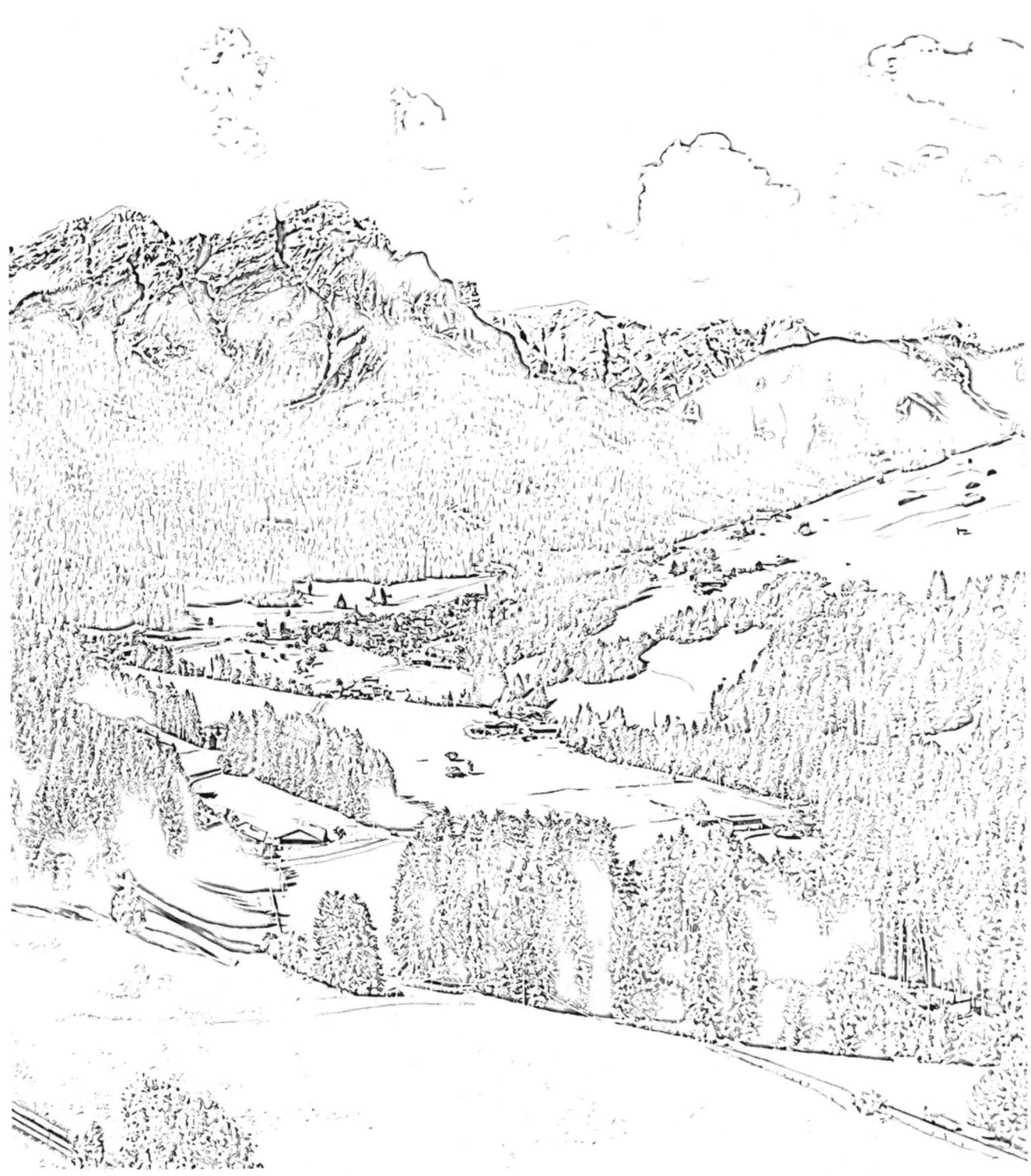

This page is intentionally left blank for bleed through

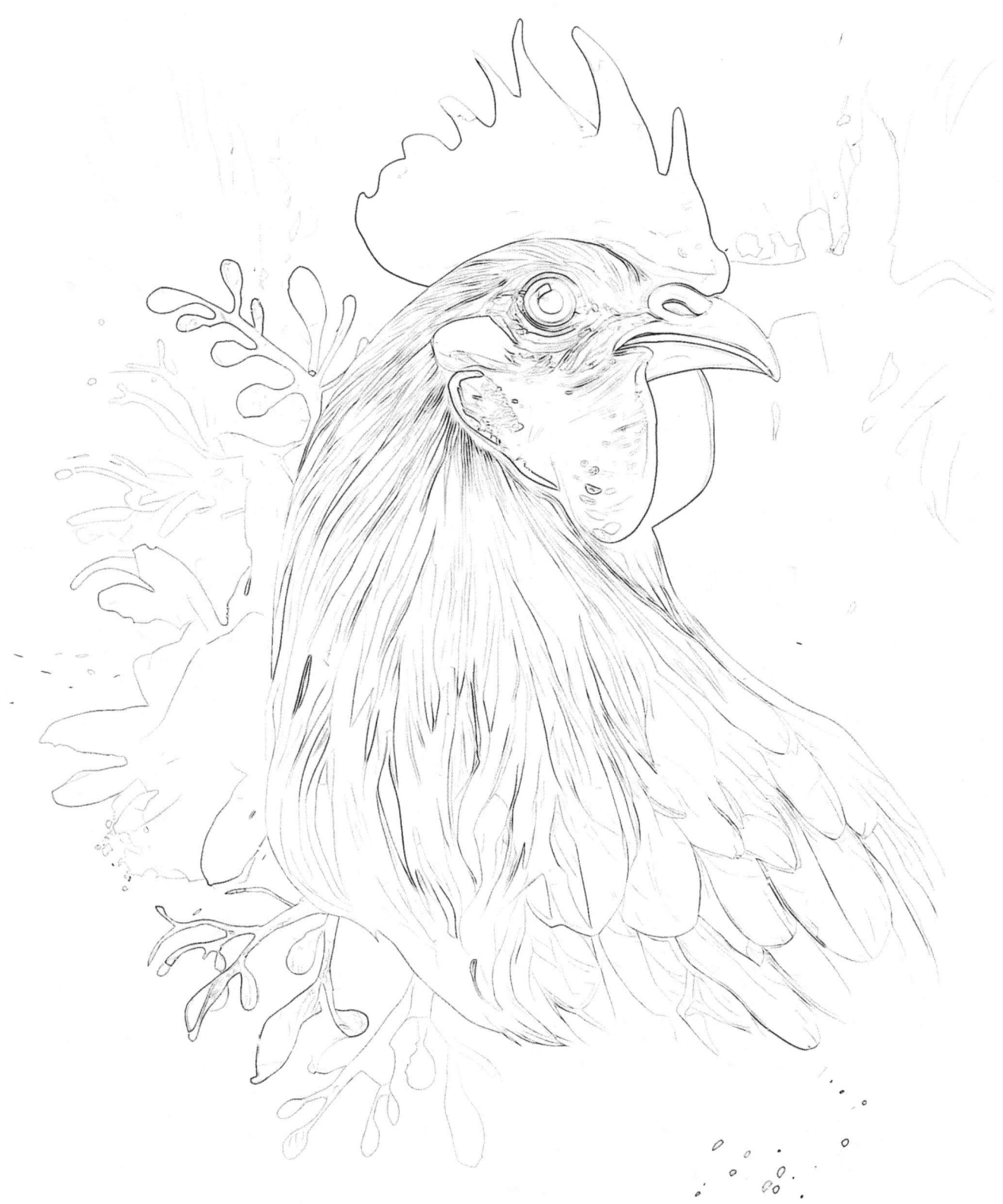

This page is intentionally left blank for bleed through

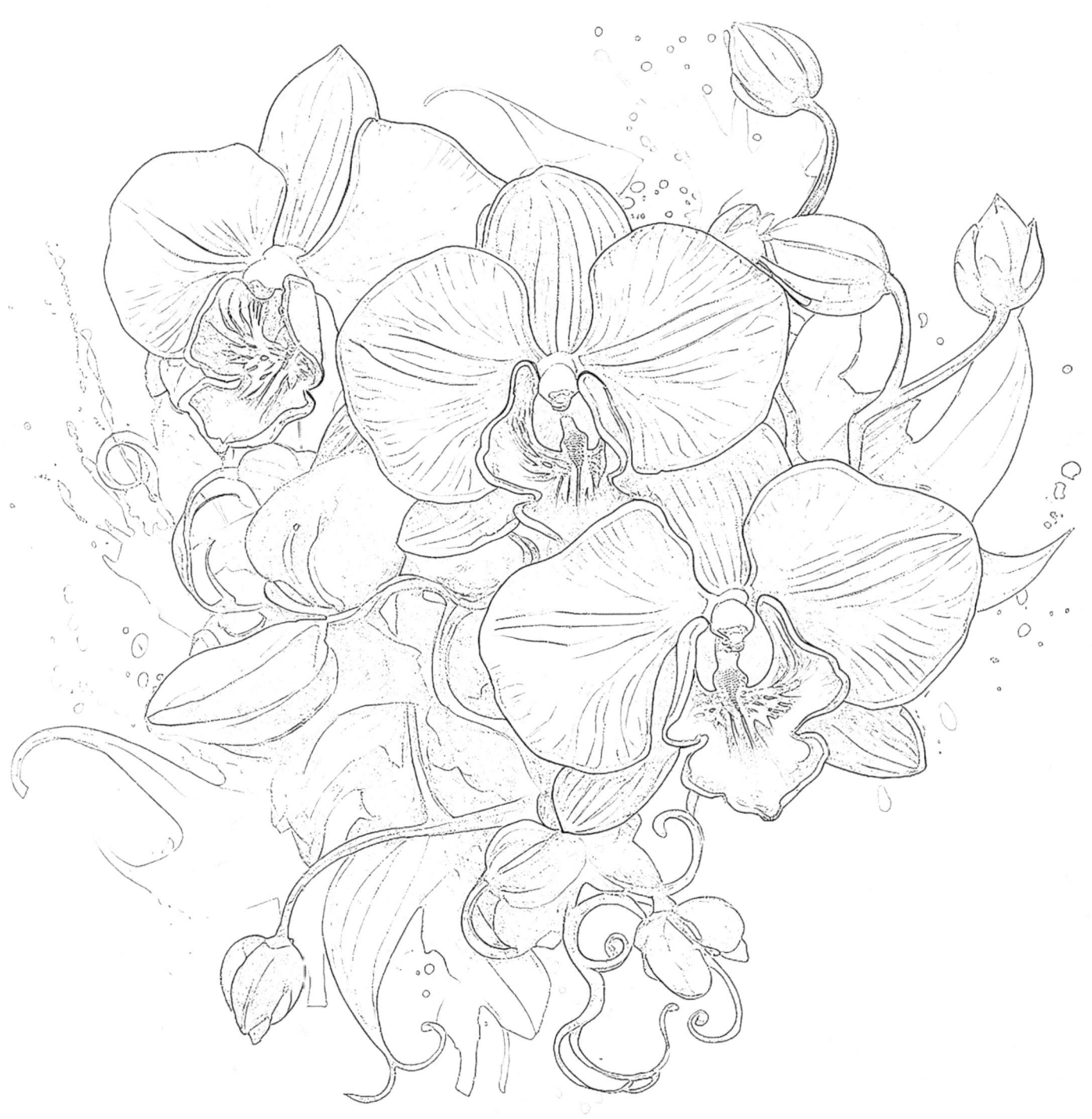

This page is intentionally left blank for bleed through

This page is intentionally left blank for bleed through

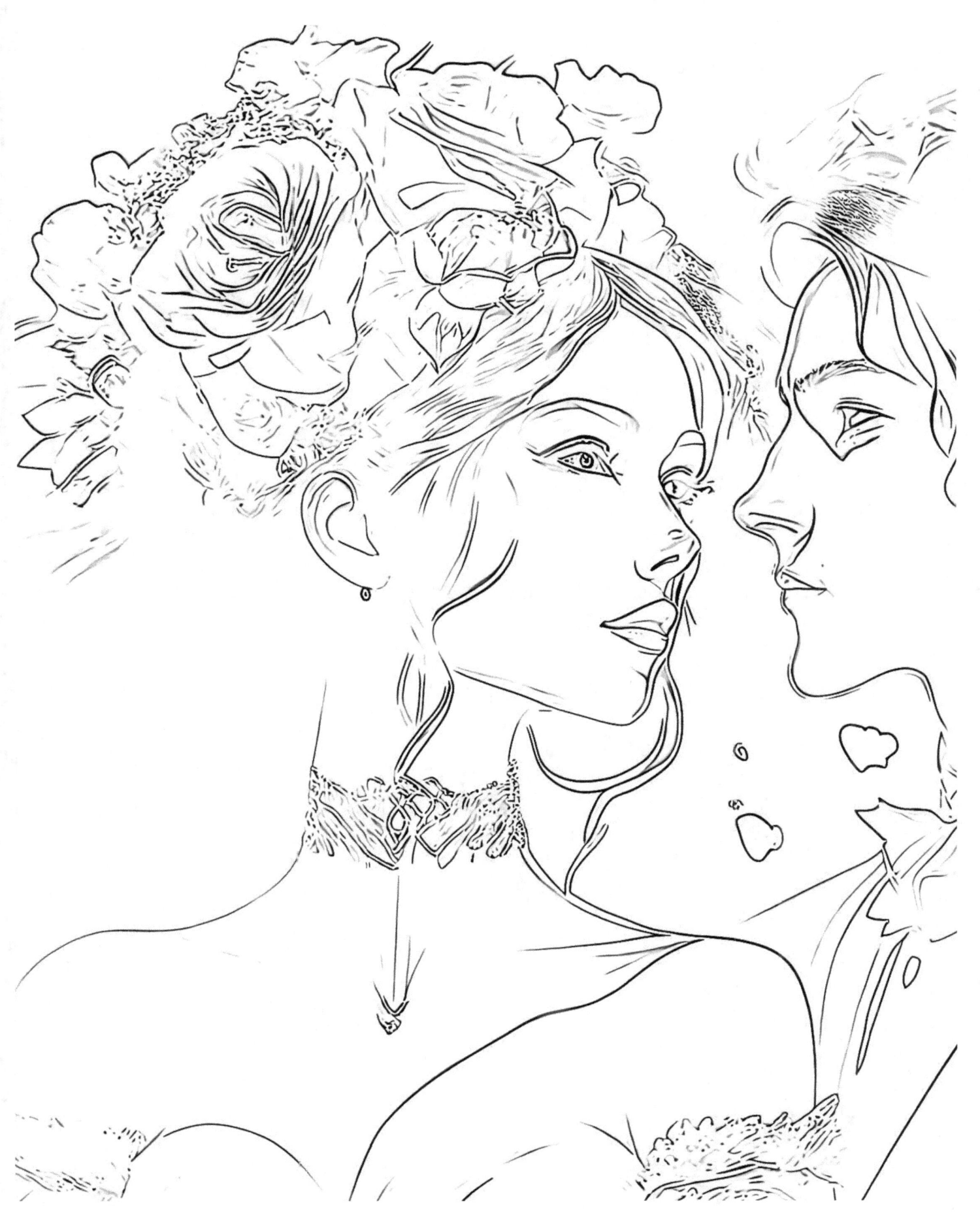

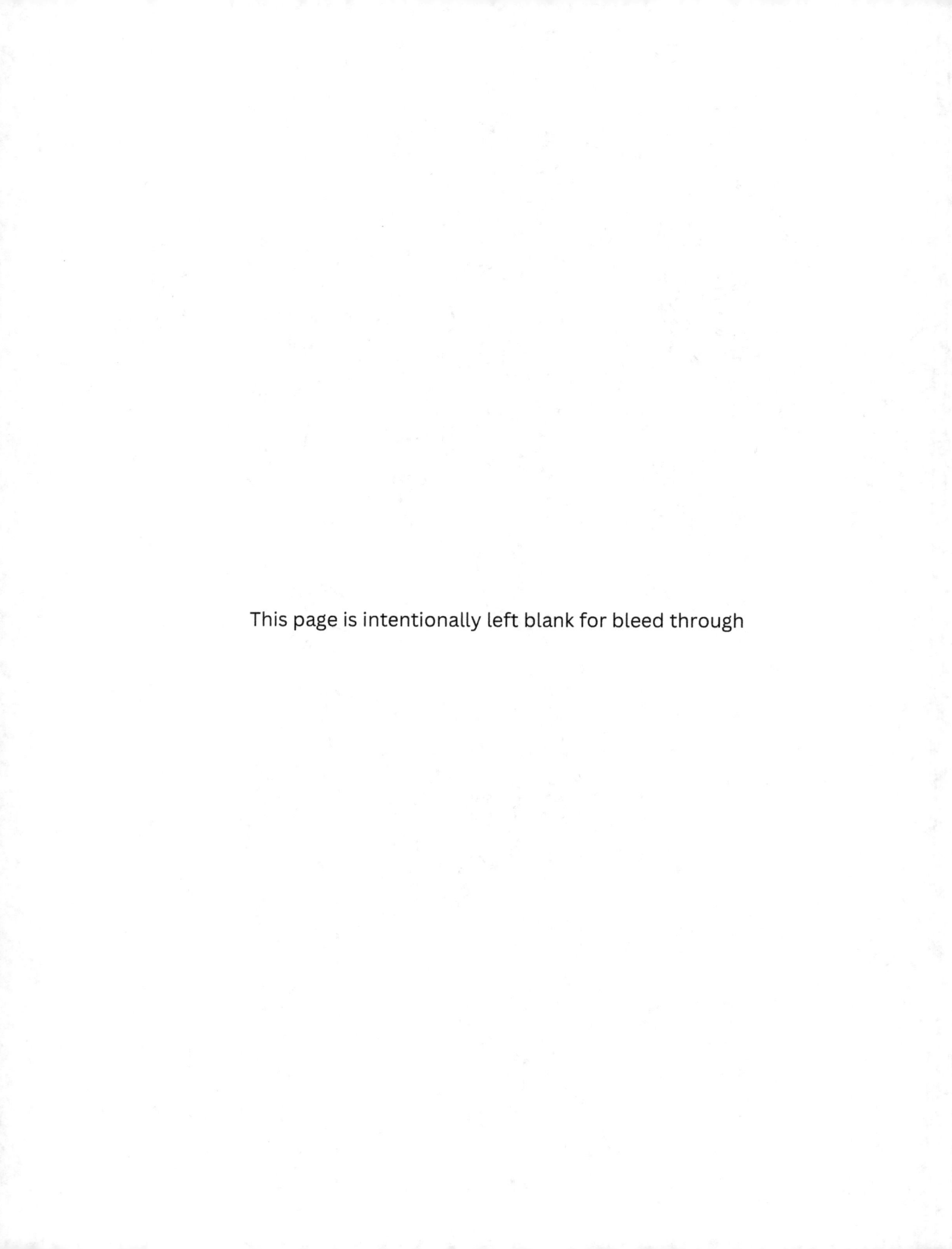

This page is intentionally left blank for bleed through

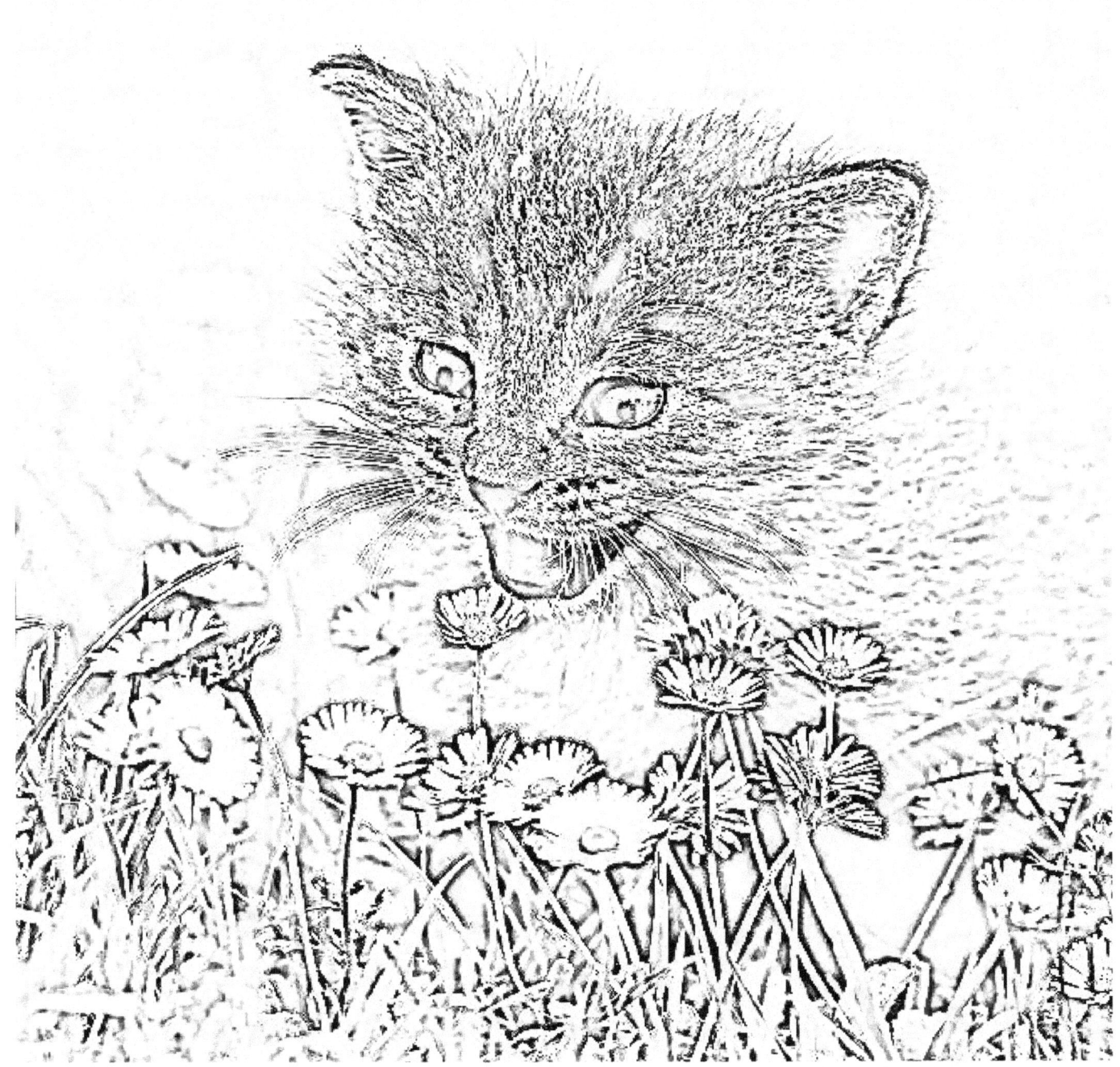

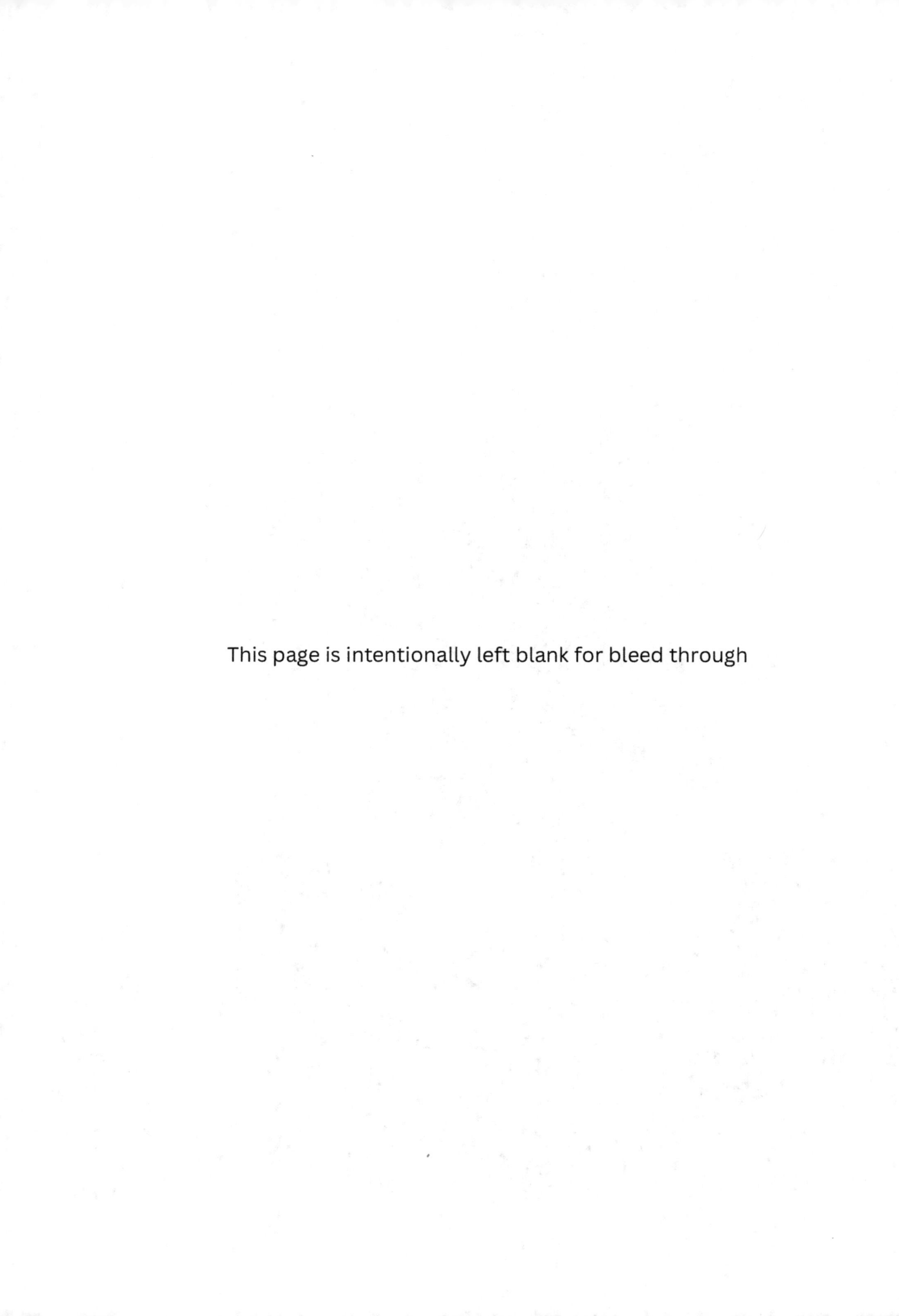

This page is intentionally left blank for bleed through

THE ELVEN PRINCE

INTERNATIONAL BESTSELLING AUTHOR

K. ROSE

This page is intentionally left blank for bleed through

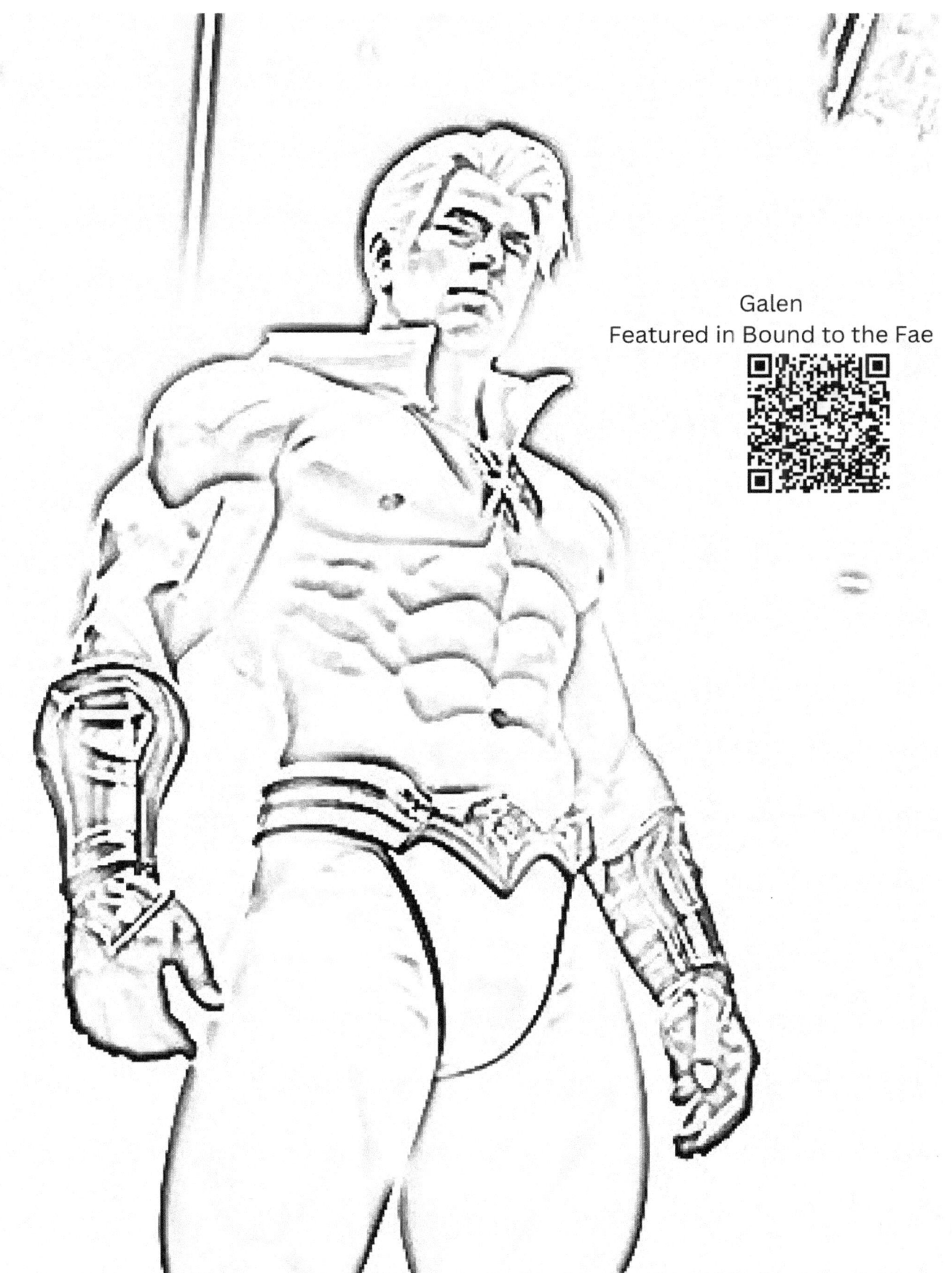

Galen
Featured in Bound to the Fae

This page is intentionally left blank for bleed through

OBSESSION

INTERNATIONAL BEST SELLING AUTHOR

K. ROSE

This page is intentionally left blank for bleed through

Who can resist a PSL ?
Start your Journey through Silver Springs Library today

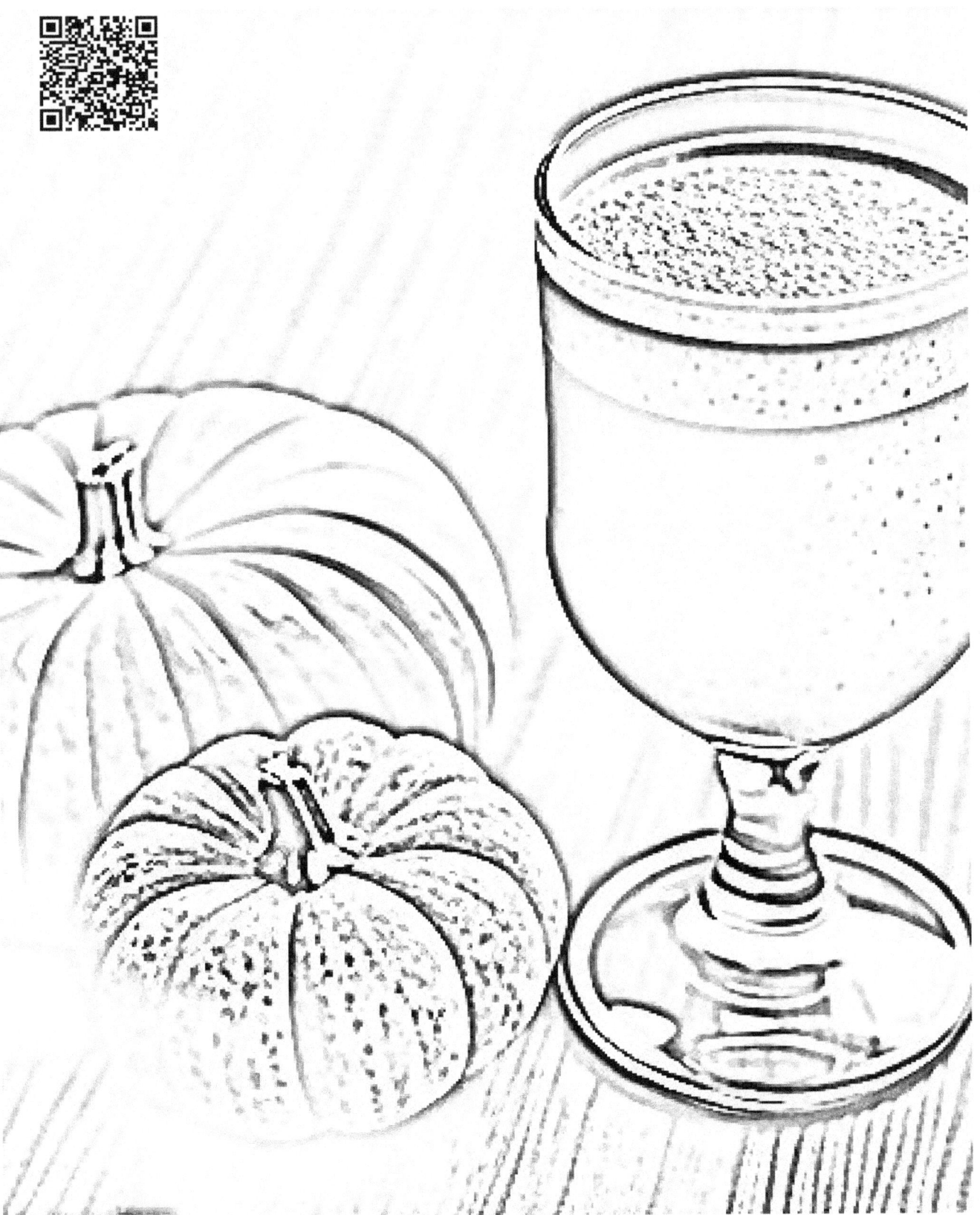

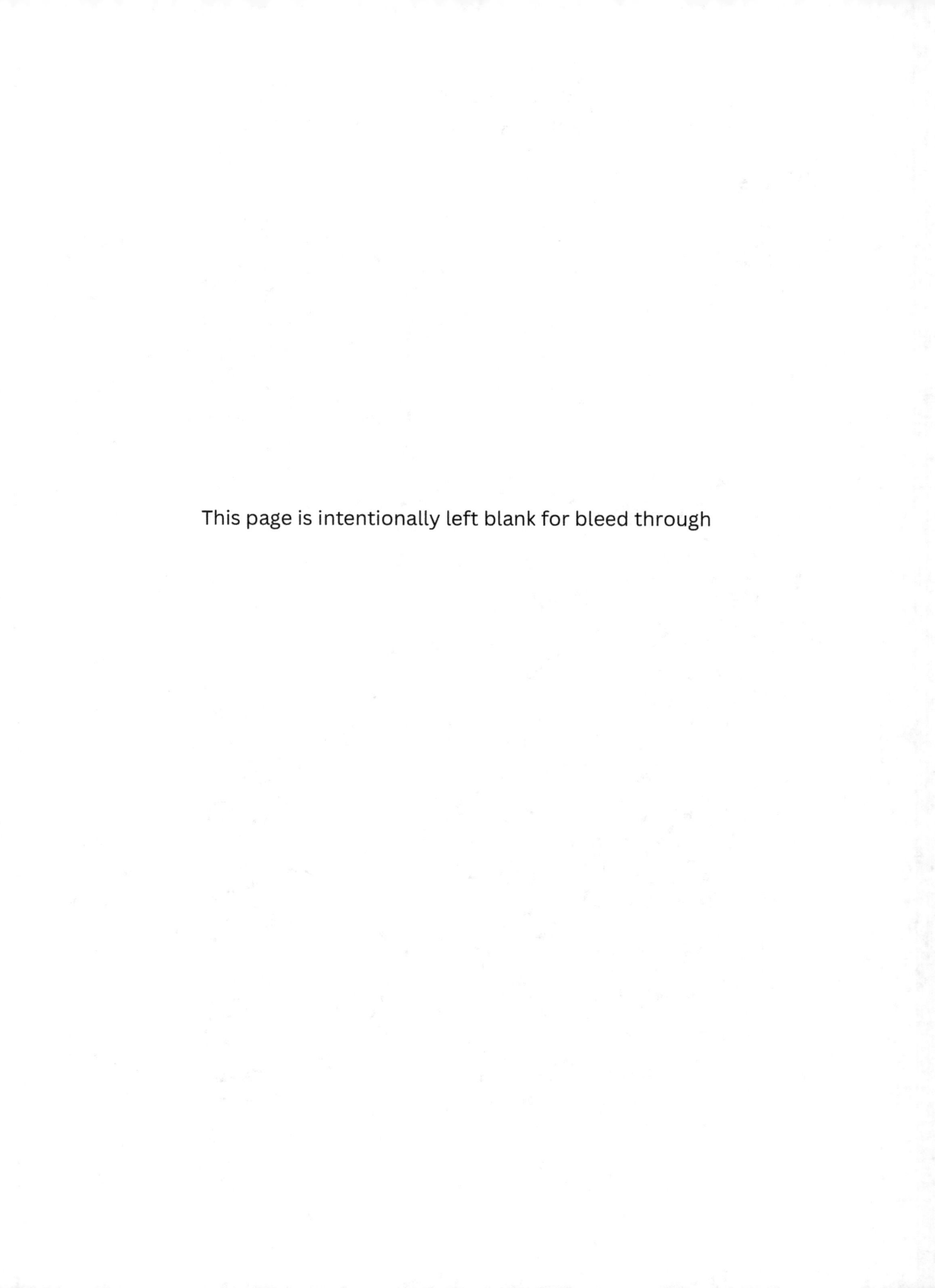

This page is intentionally left blank for bleed through

THE PROPHECY OF
THE WATER
SPRITE

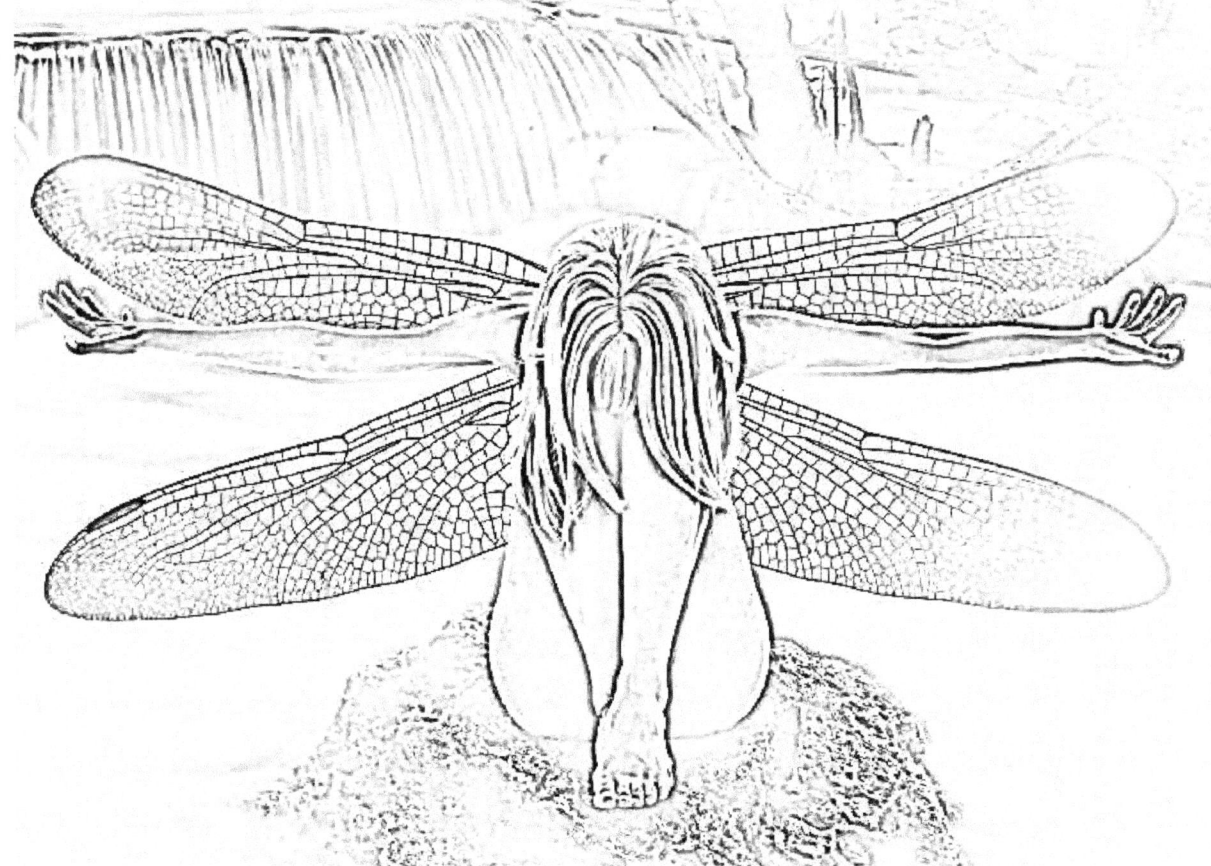

K ROSE

This page is intentionally left blank for bleed through

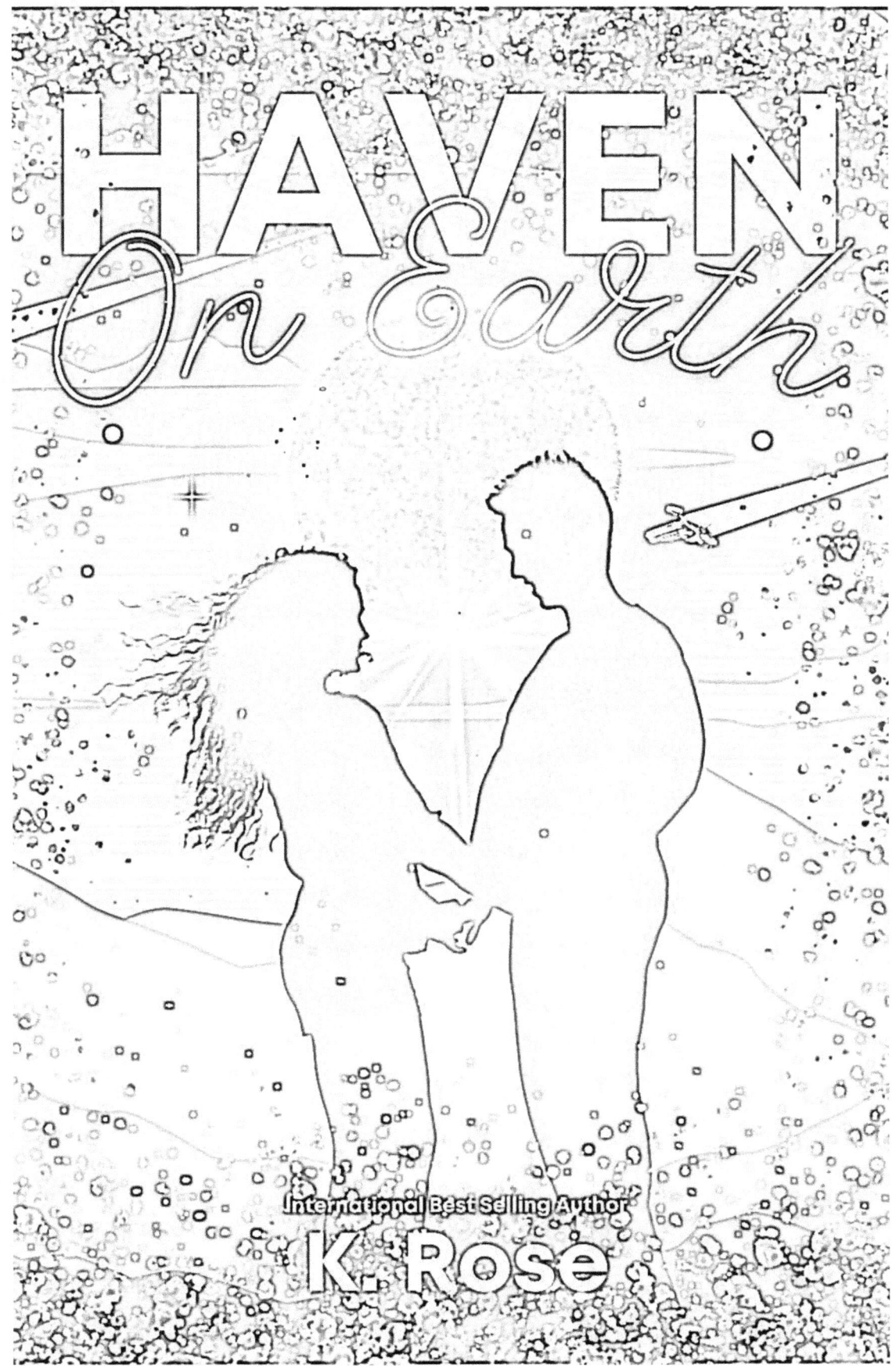

HAVEN
On Earth

International Best Selling Author
K. Rose

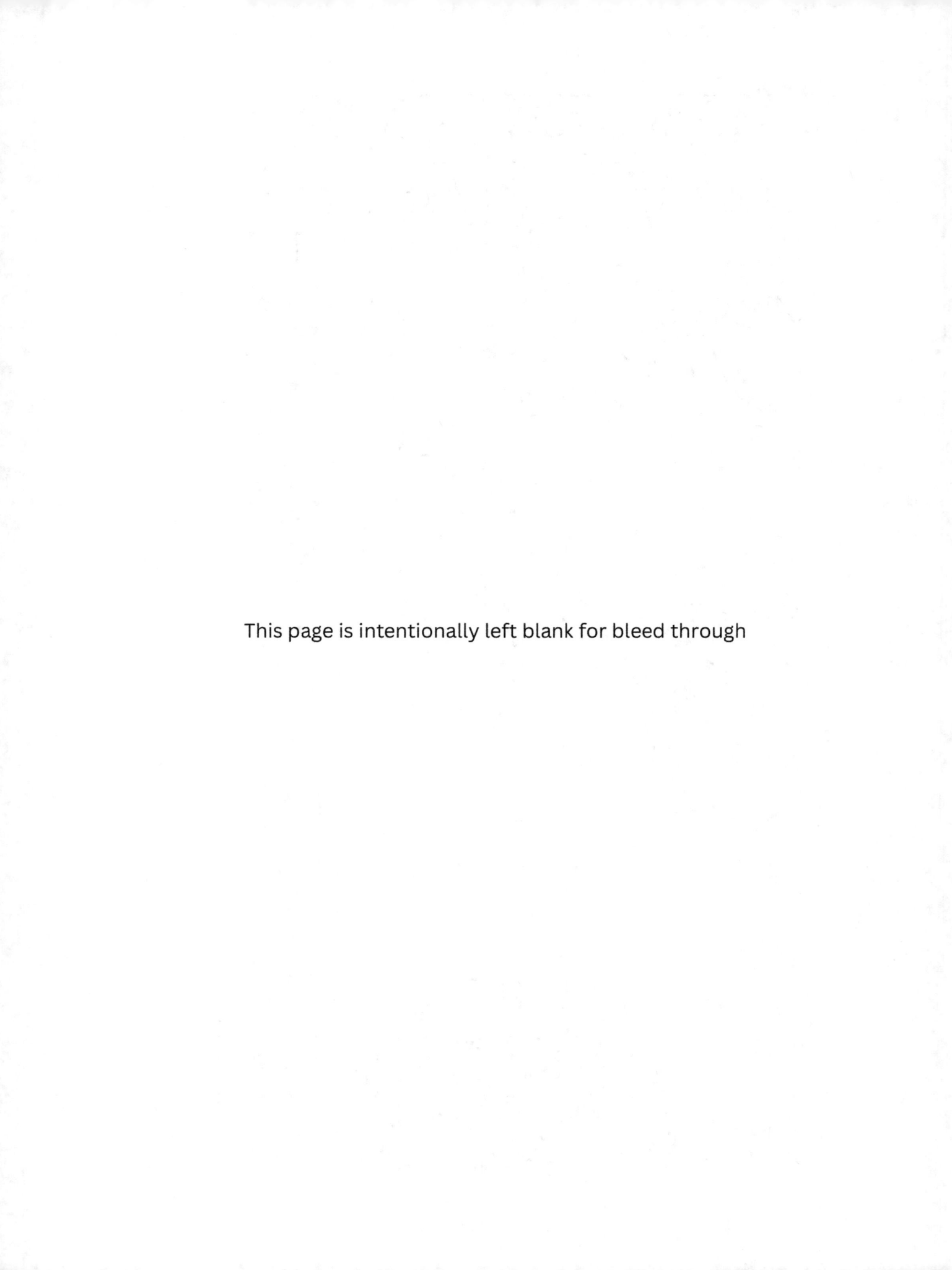

This page is intentionally left blank for bleed through

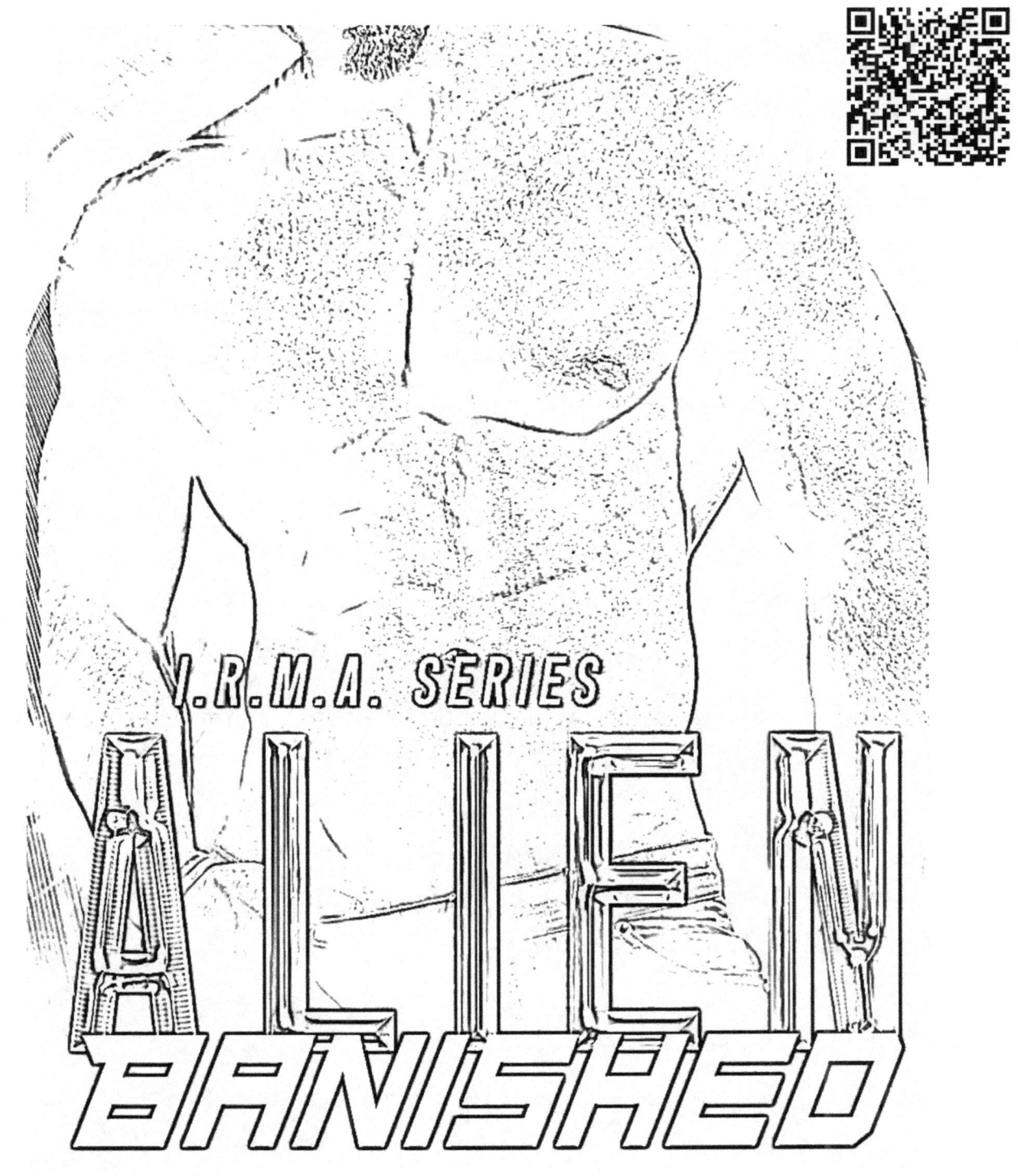

I.R.M.A. SERIES

ALIEN
BANISHED

INTERNATIONAL BESTSELLING AUTHOR
K. ROSE

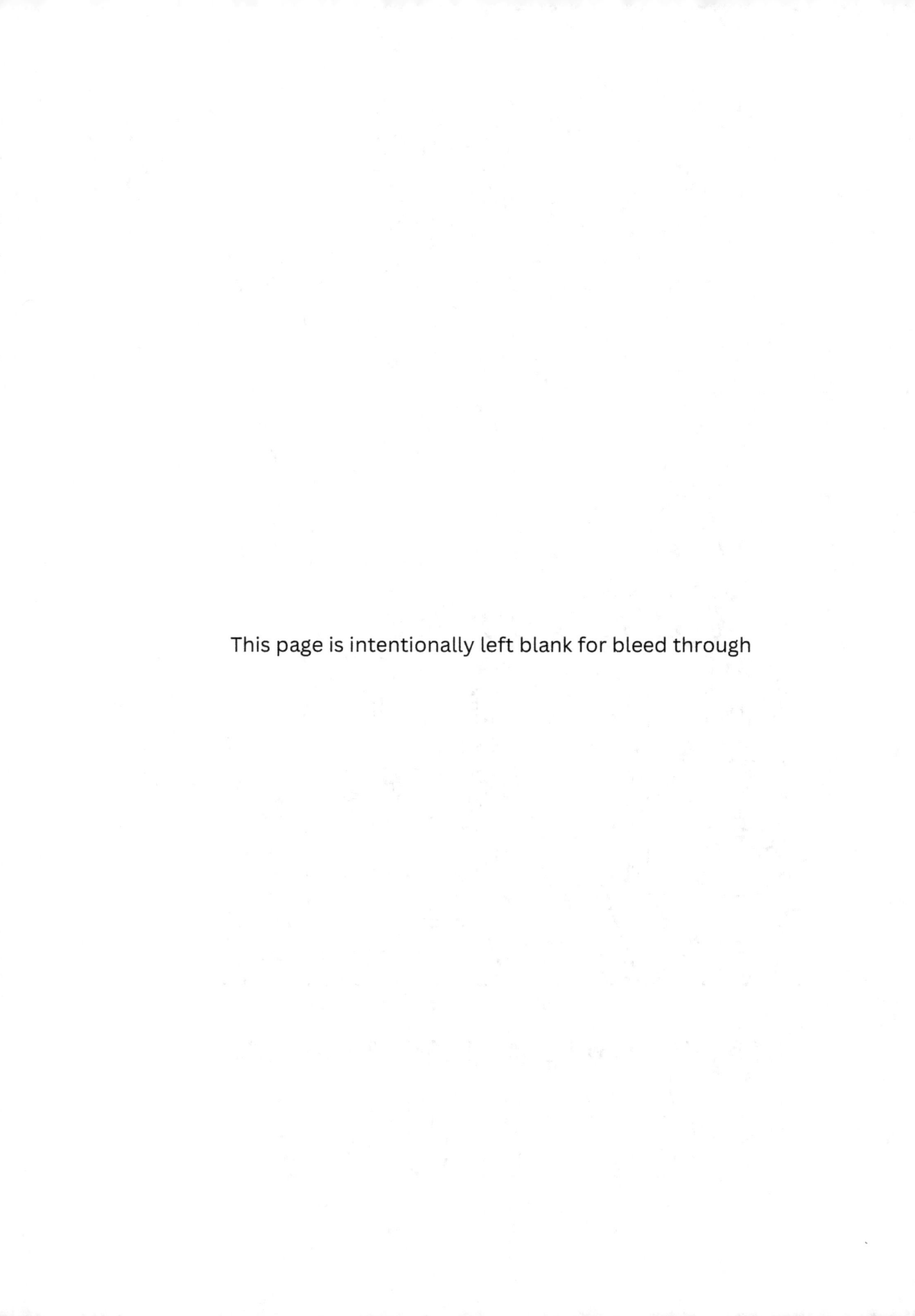

This page is intentionally left blank for bleed through

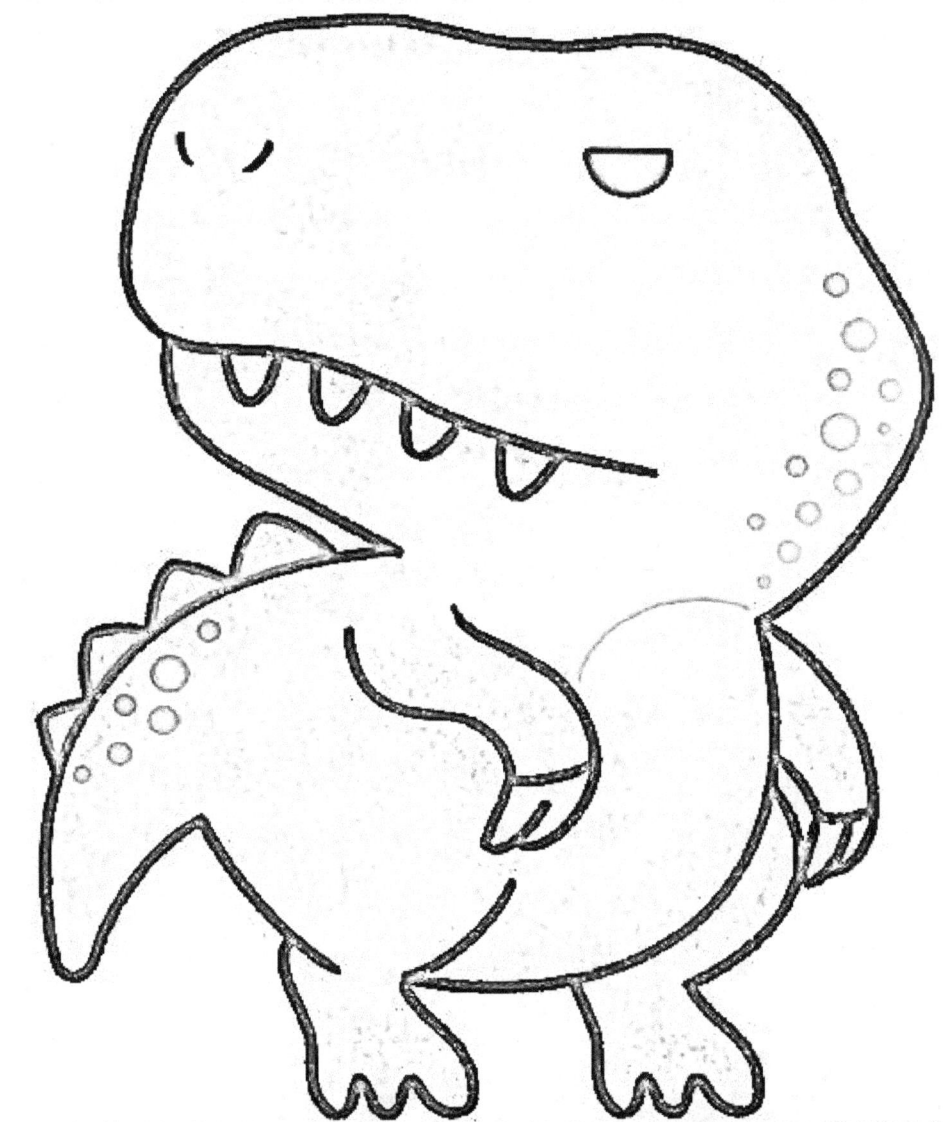

IF YOU'RE HAPPY AND YOU KNOW IT
CLAP YOUR....OH.

This page is intentionally left blank for bleed through

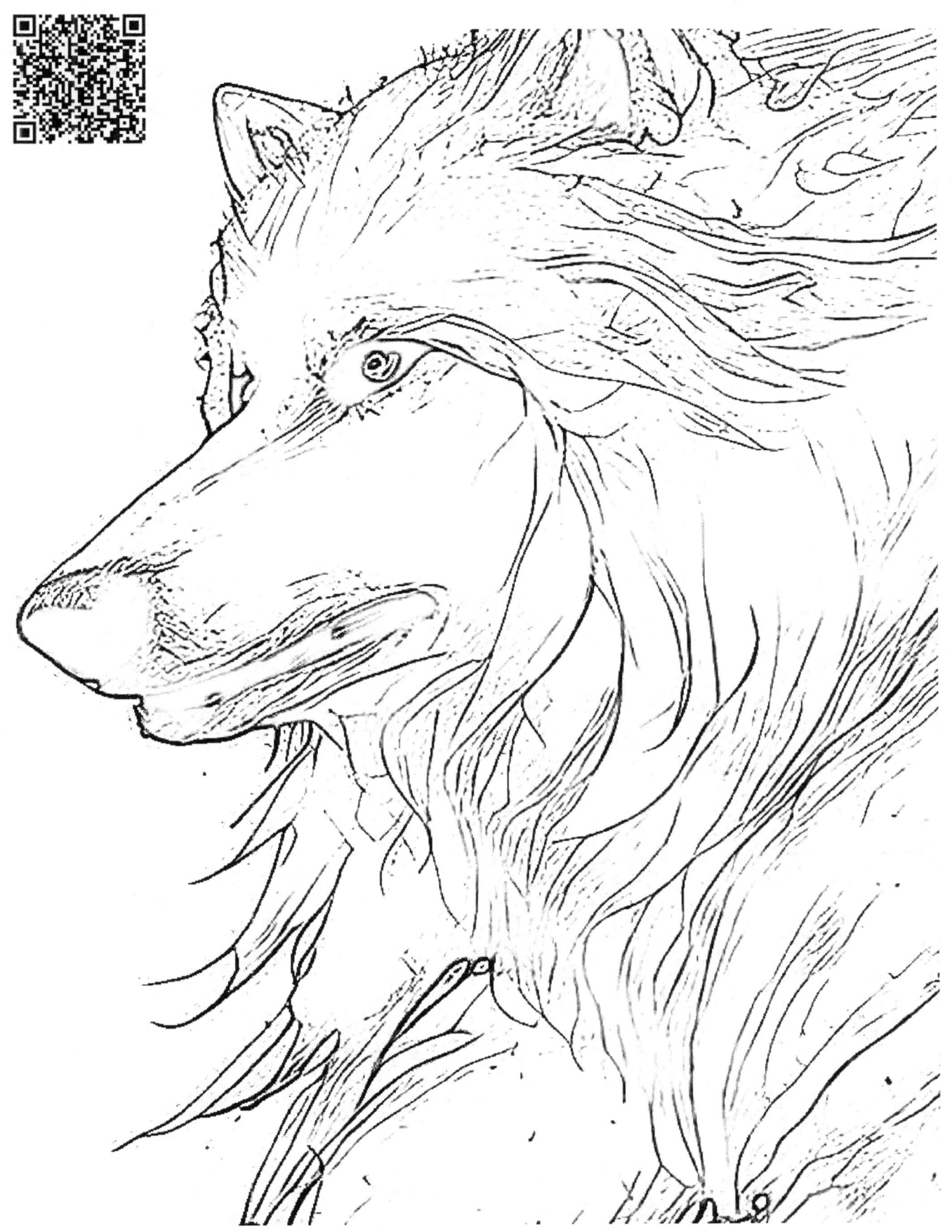

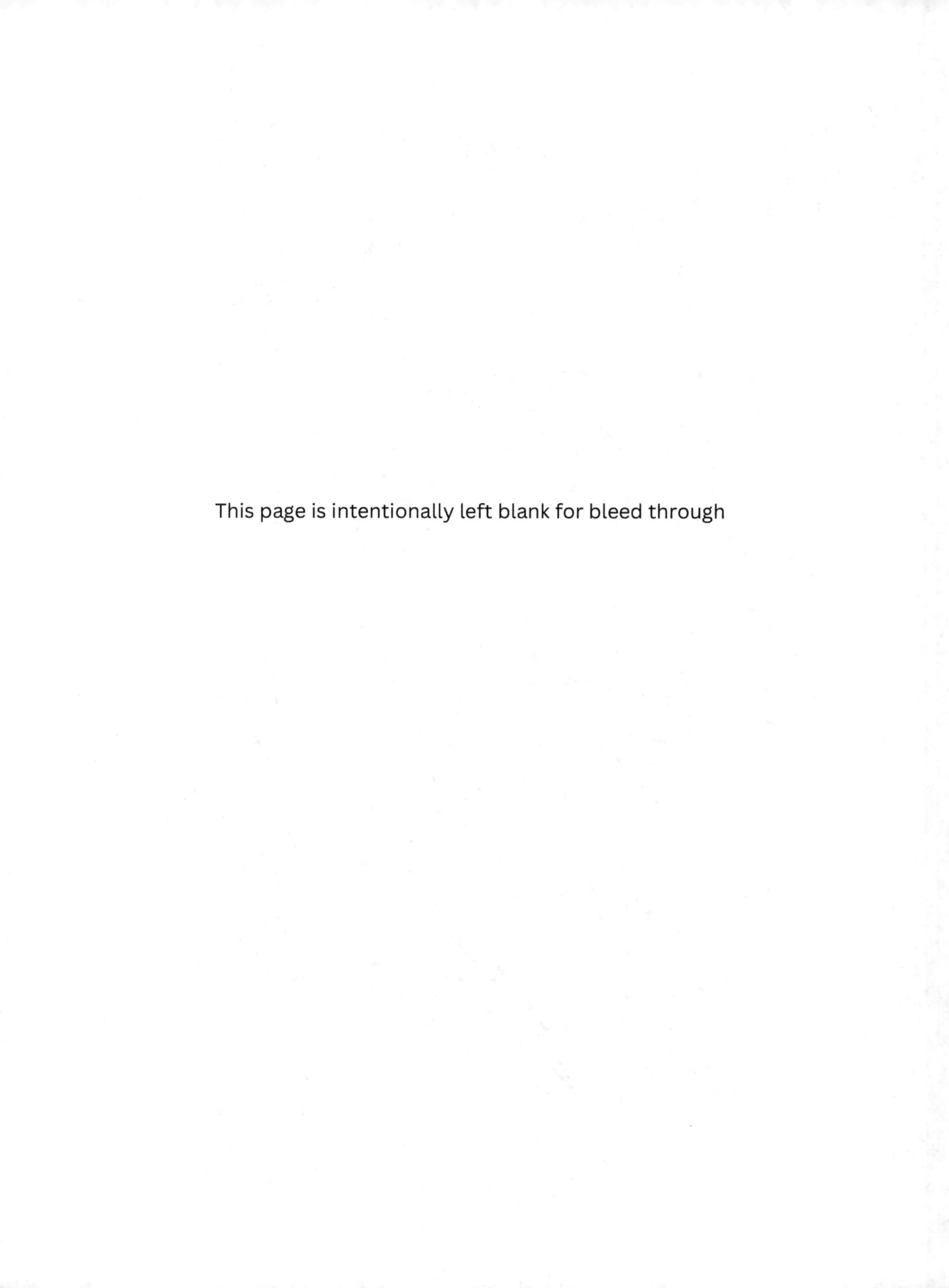

This page is intentionally left blank for bleed through

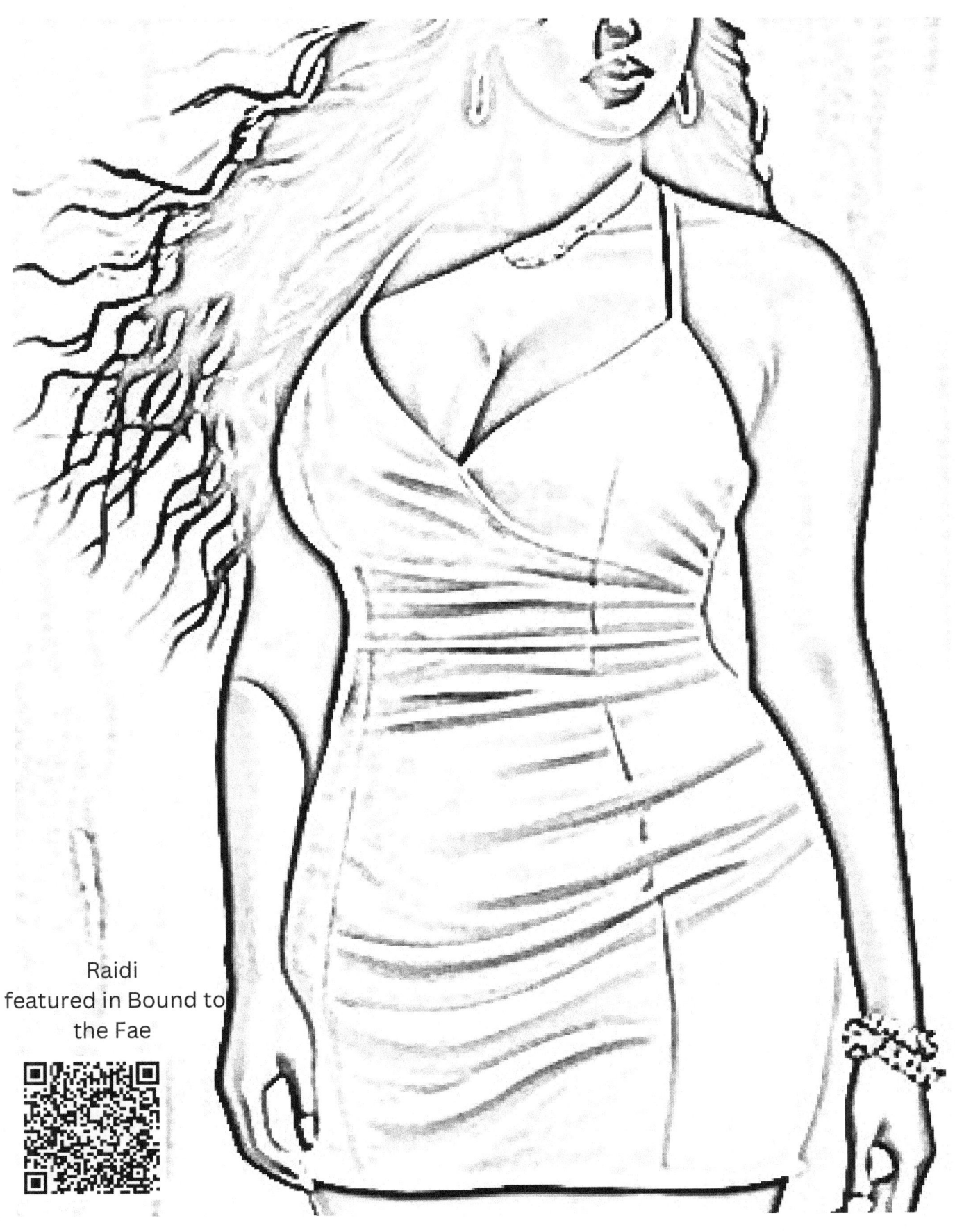

Raidi
featured in Bound to
the Fae

This page is intentionally left blank for bleed through

Midas Touch

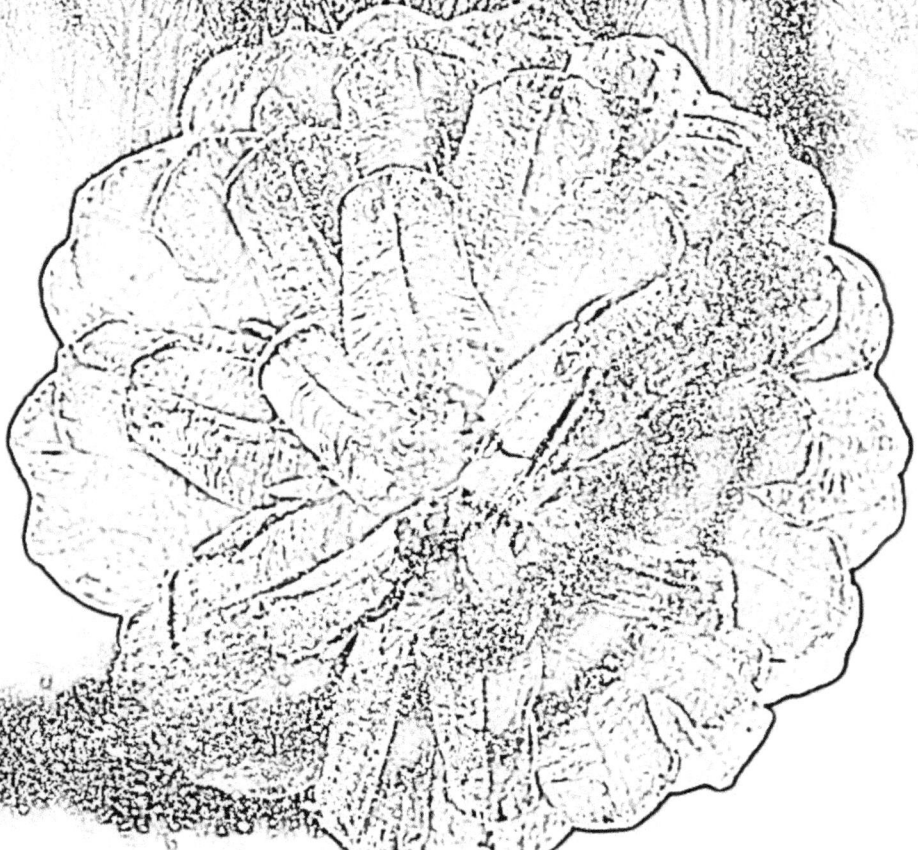

International Best Selling Author

K. Rose

This page is intentionally left blank for bleed through

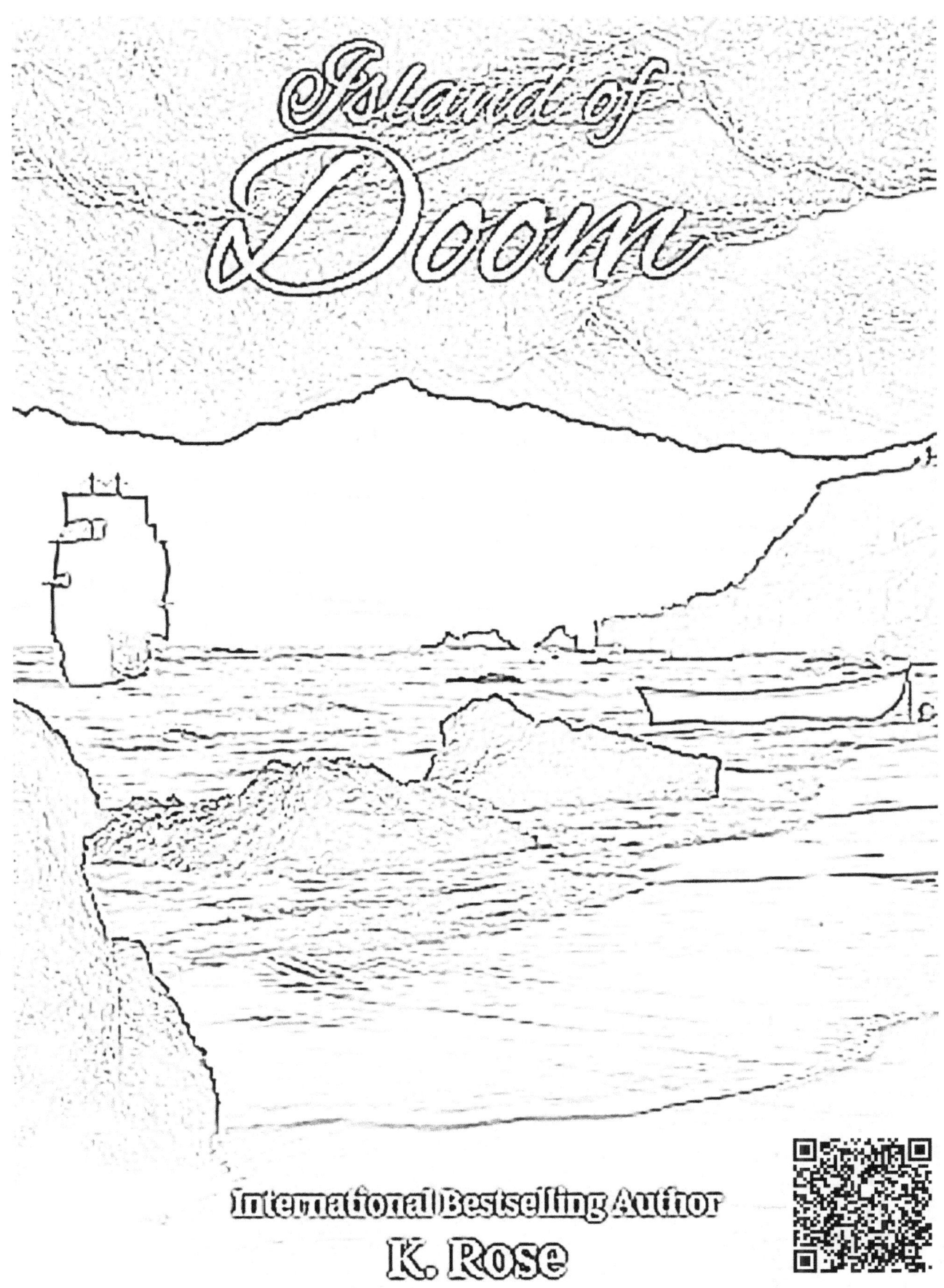

Island of Doom

International Bestselling Author

K. Rose

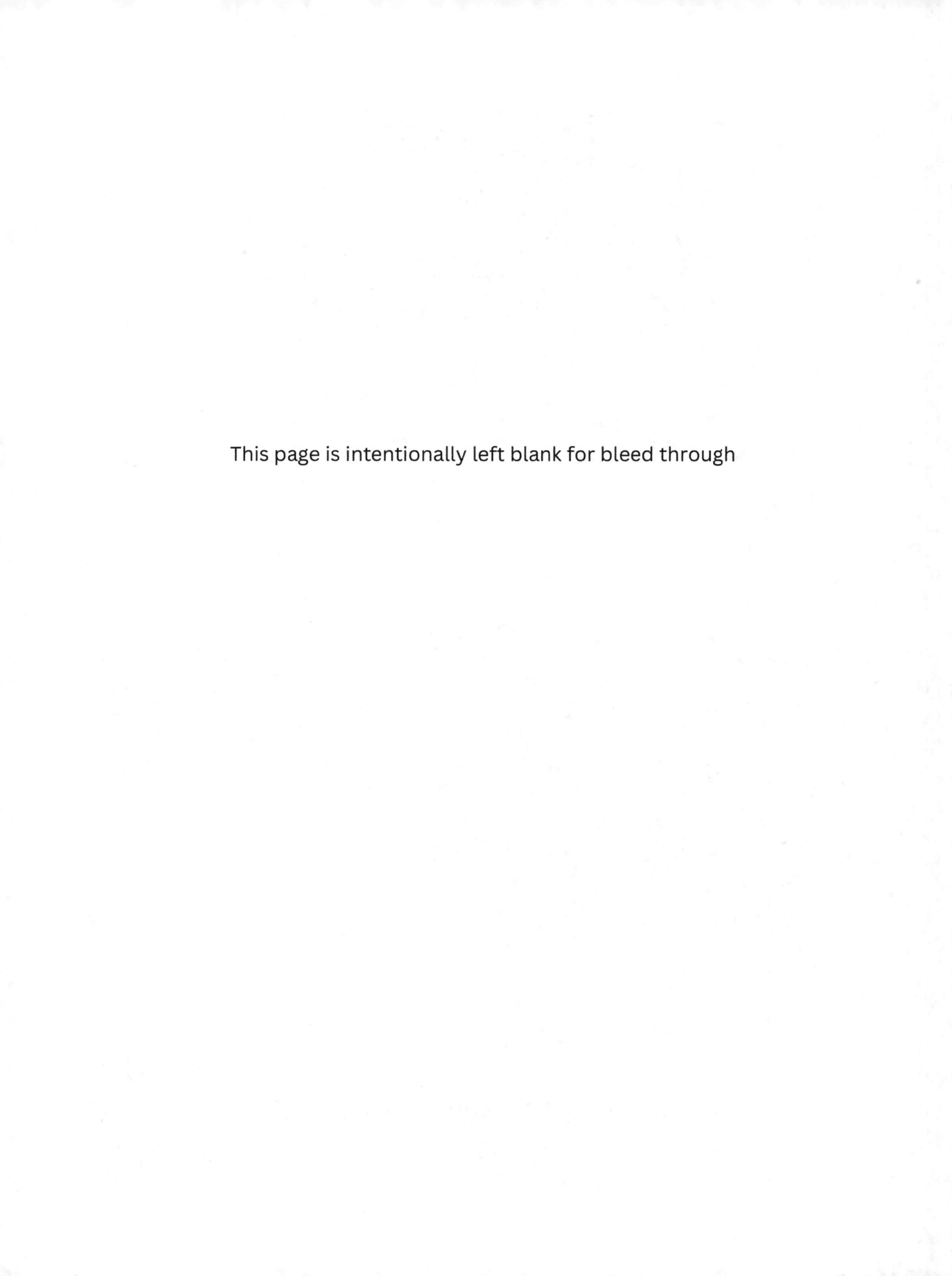

This page is intentionally left blank for bleed through

Flying Huntress

K. Rose

This page is intentionally left blank for bleed through

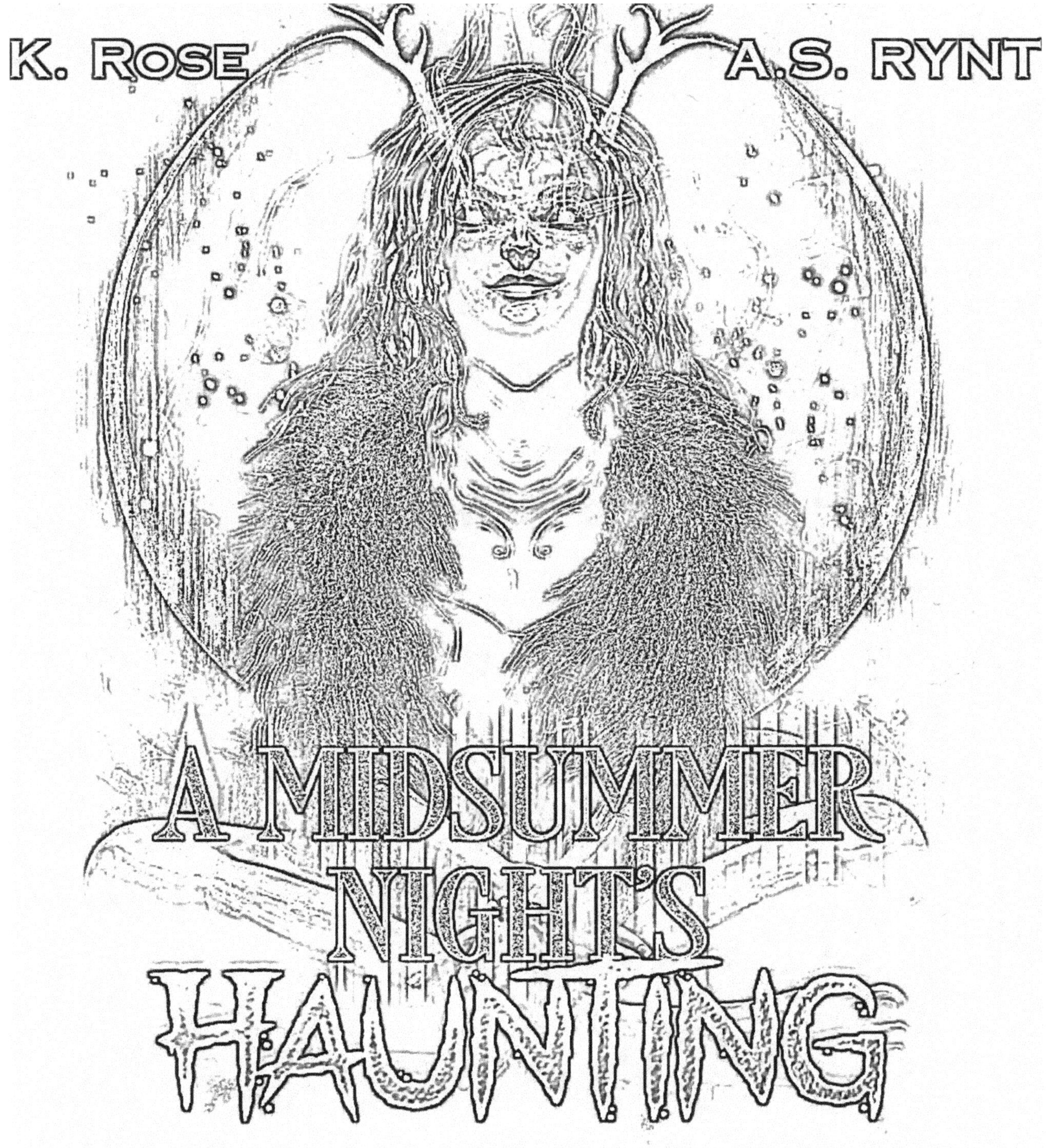

K. ROSE   A.S. RYNT

A MIDSUMMER NIGHT'S HAUNTING

This page is intentionally left blank for bleed through

The Jade Mystery

International Bestselling Author
K. ROSE

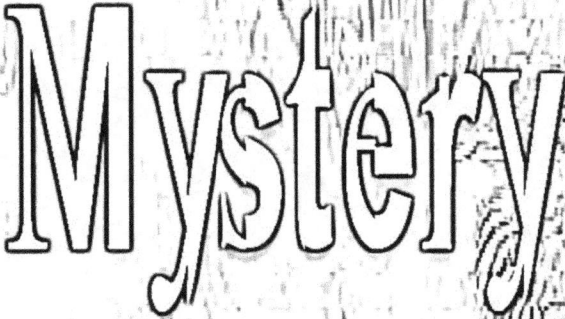
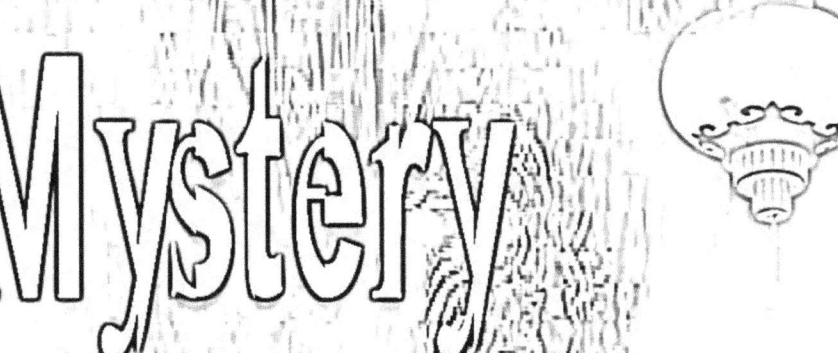

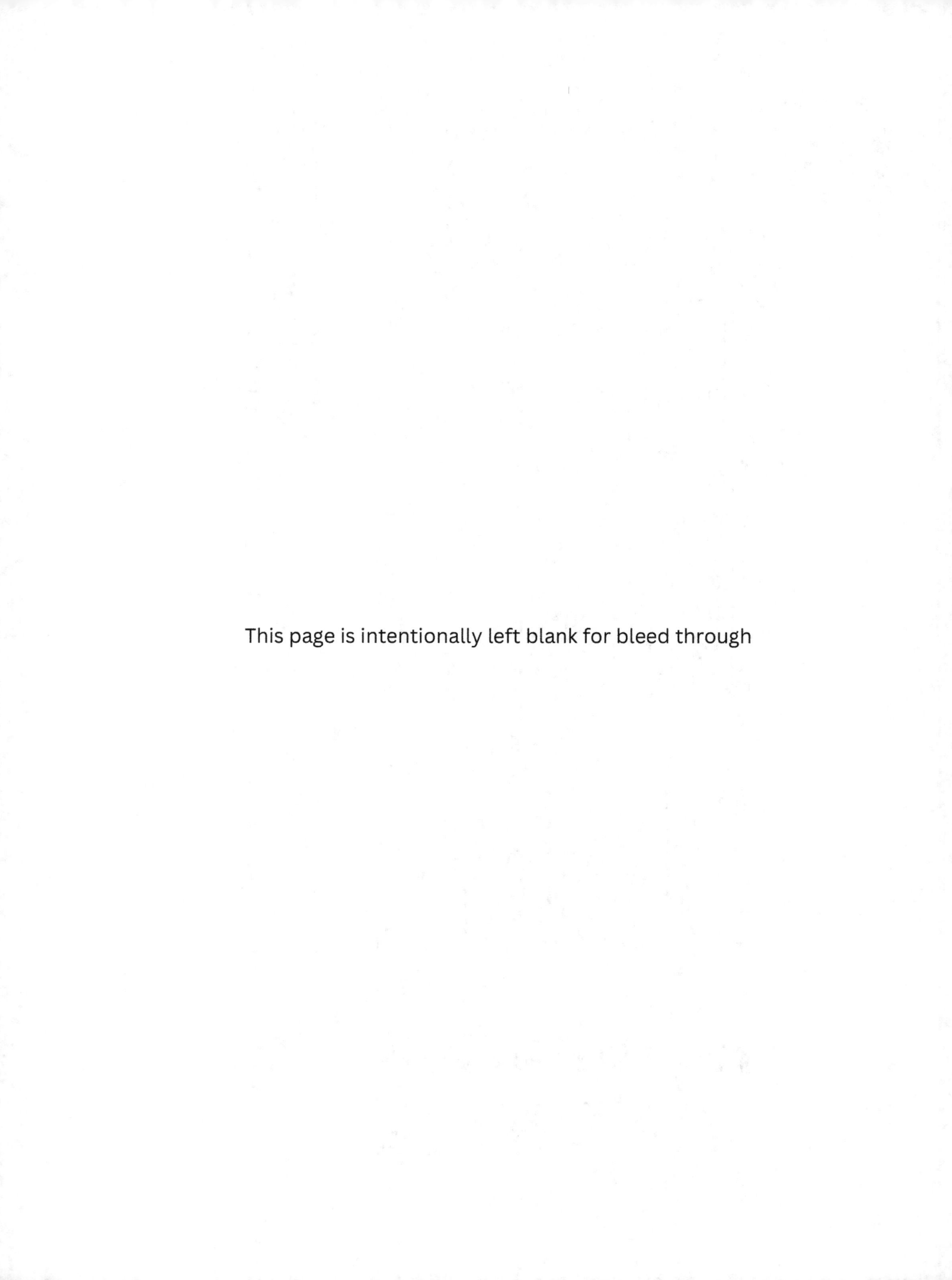

This page is intentionally left blank for bleed through

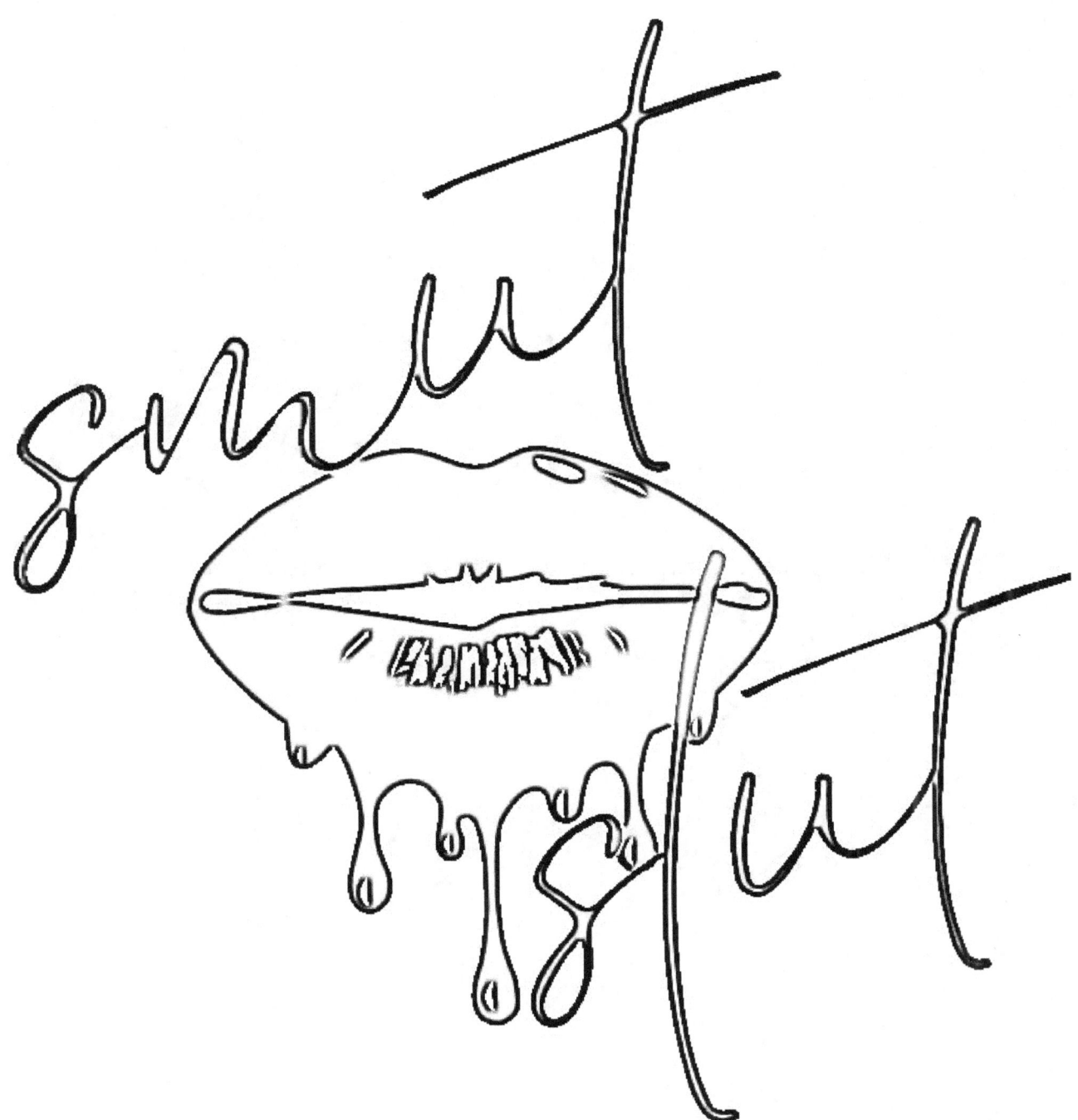

This page is intentionally left blank for bleed through

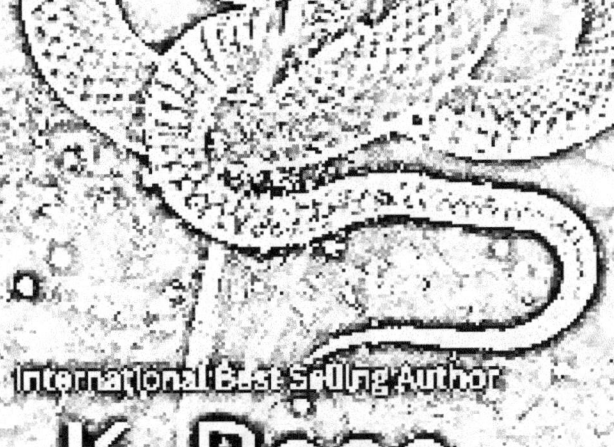

Anthology of
Strange Stories

International Best Selling Author

K. Rose

This page is intentionally left blank for bleed through

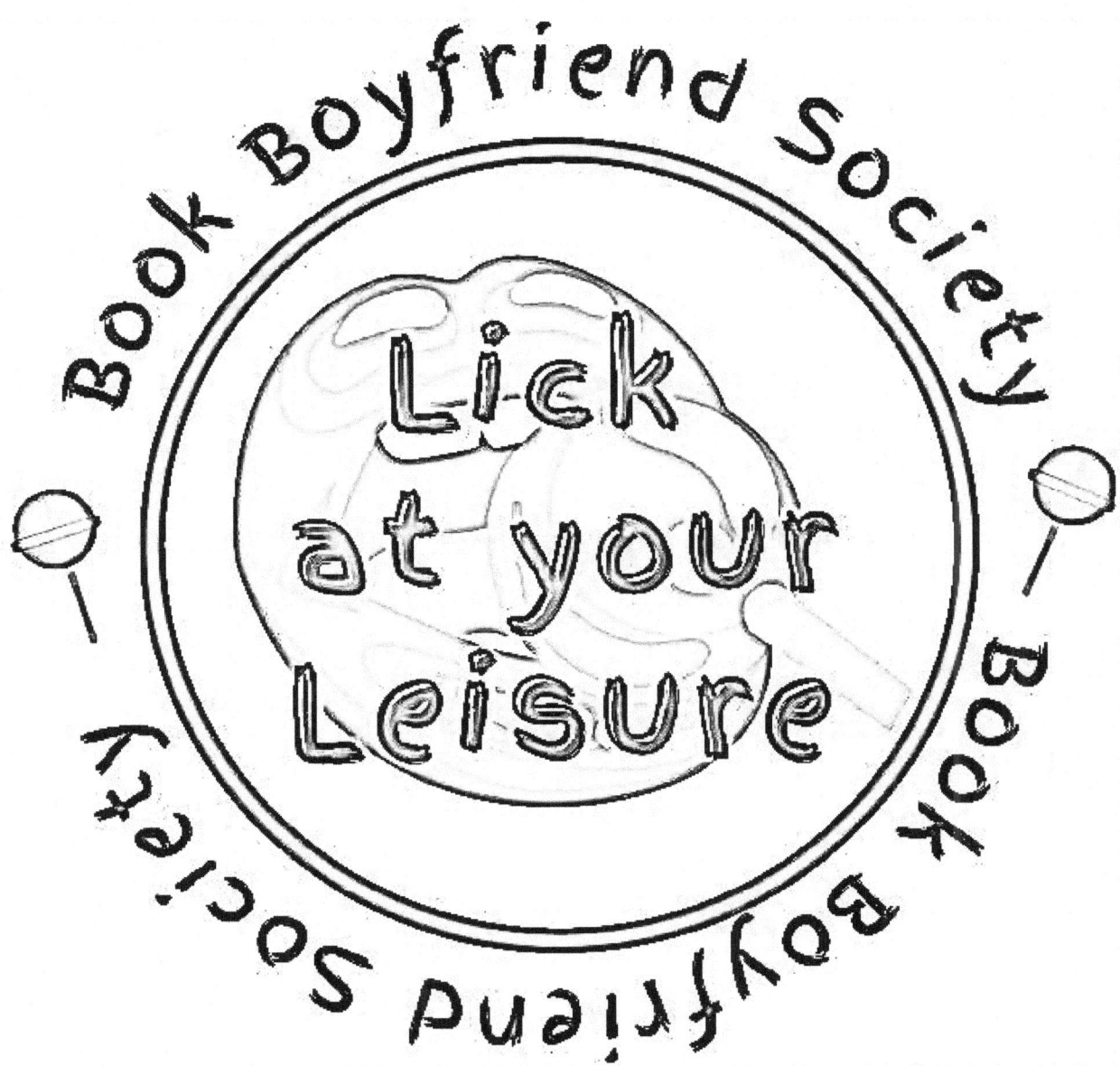

This page is intentionally left blank for bleed through

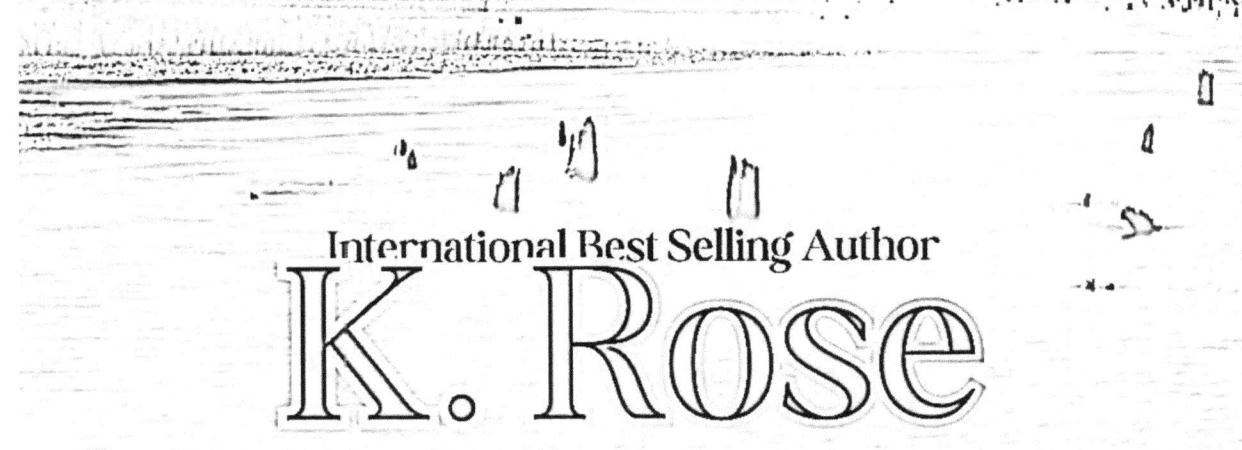

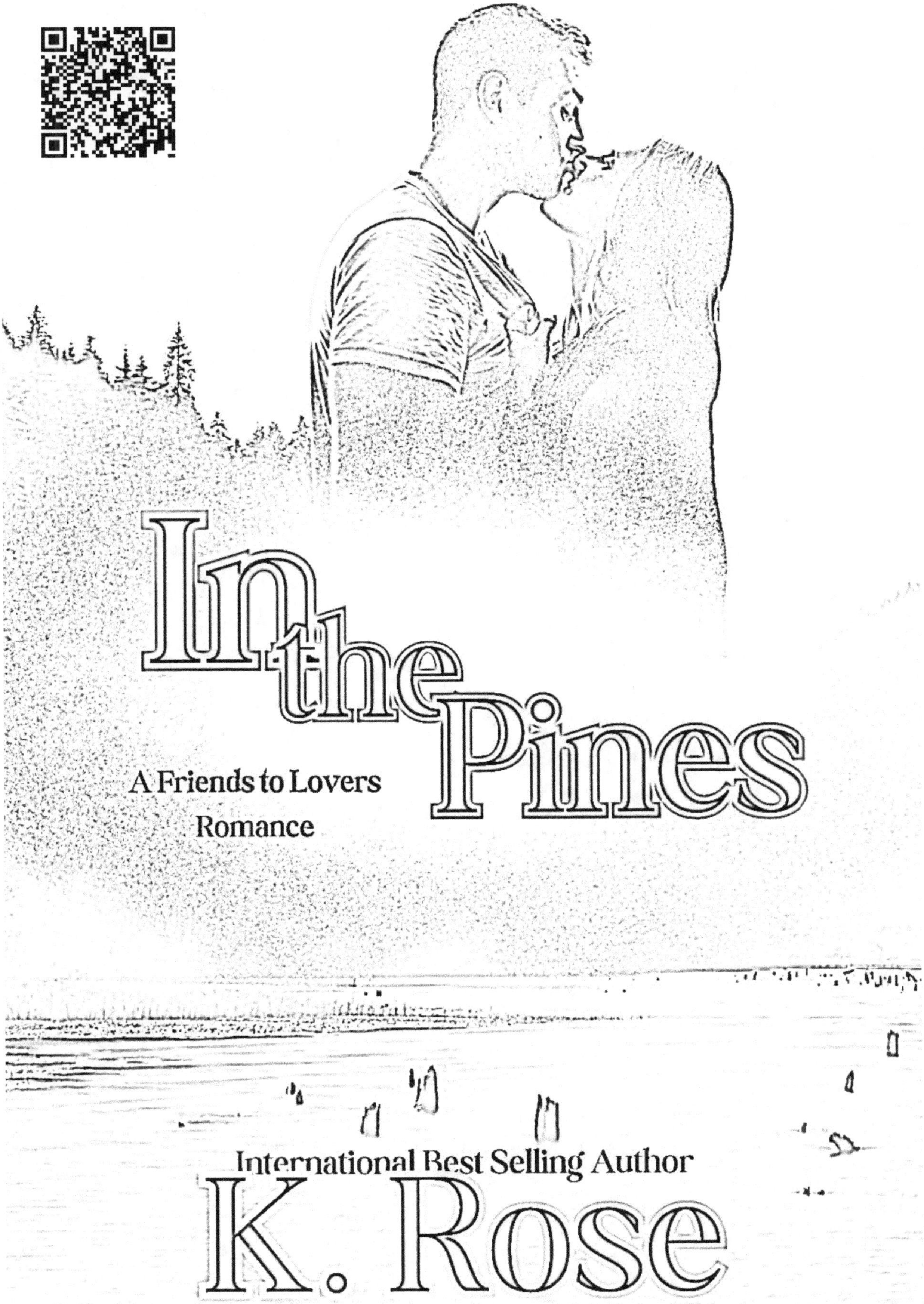

In the Pines

A Friends to Lovers
Romance

International Best Selling Author
K. Rose

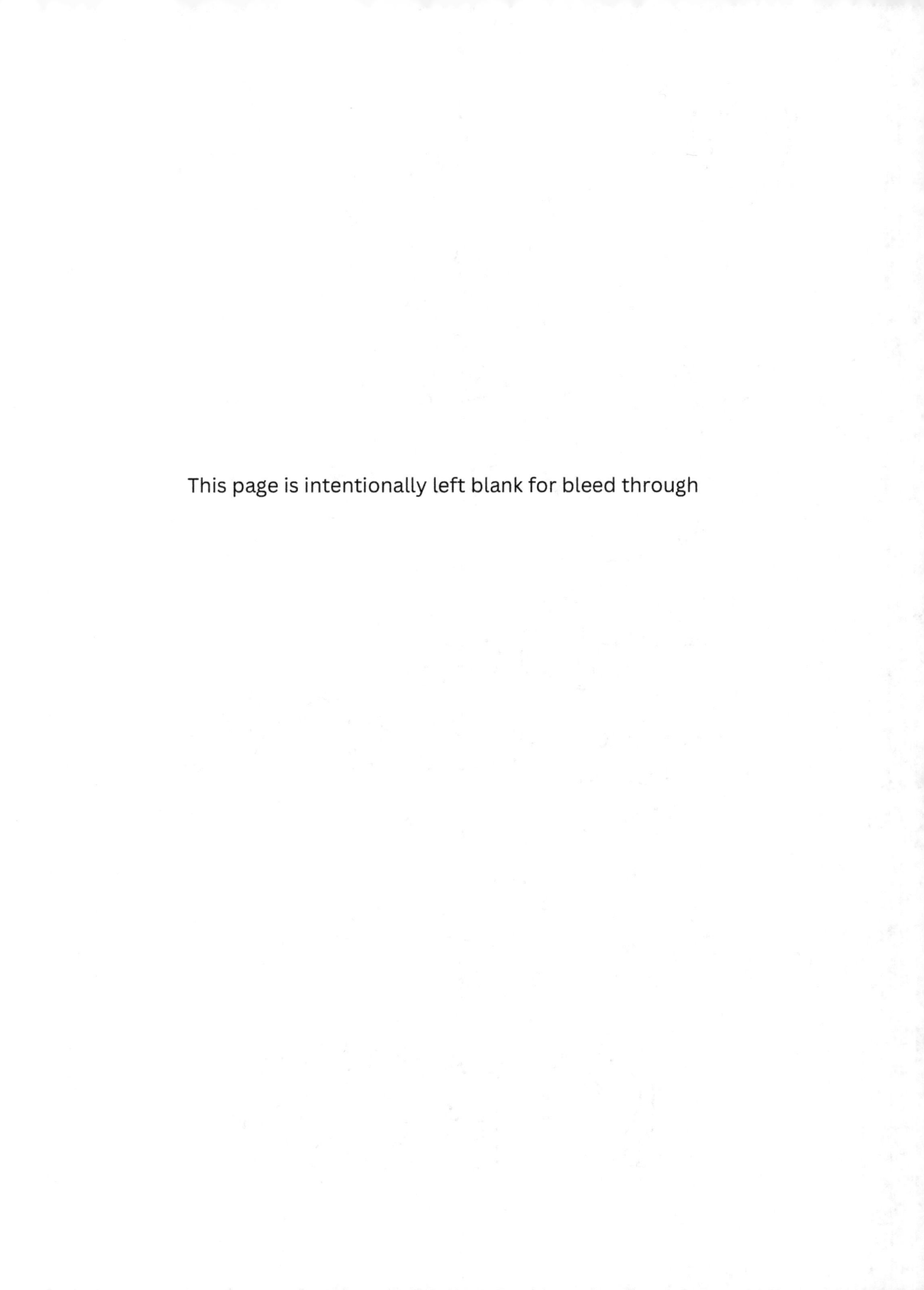

This page is intentionally left blank for bleed through

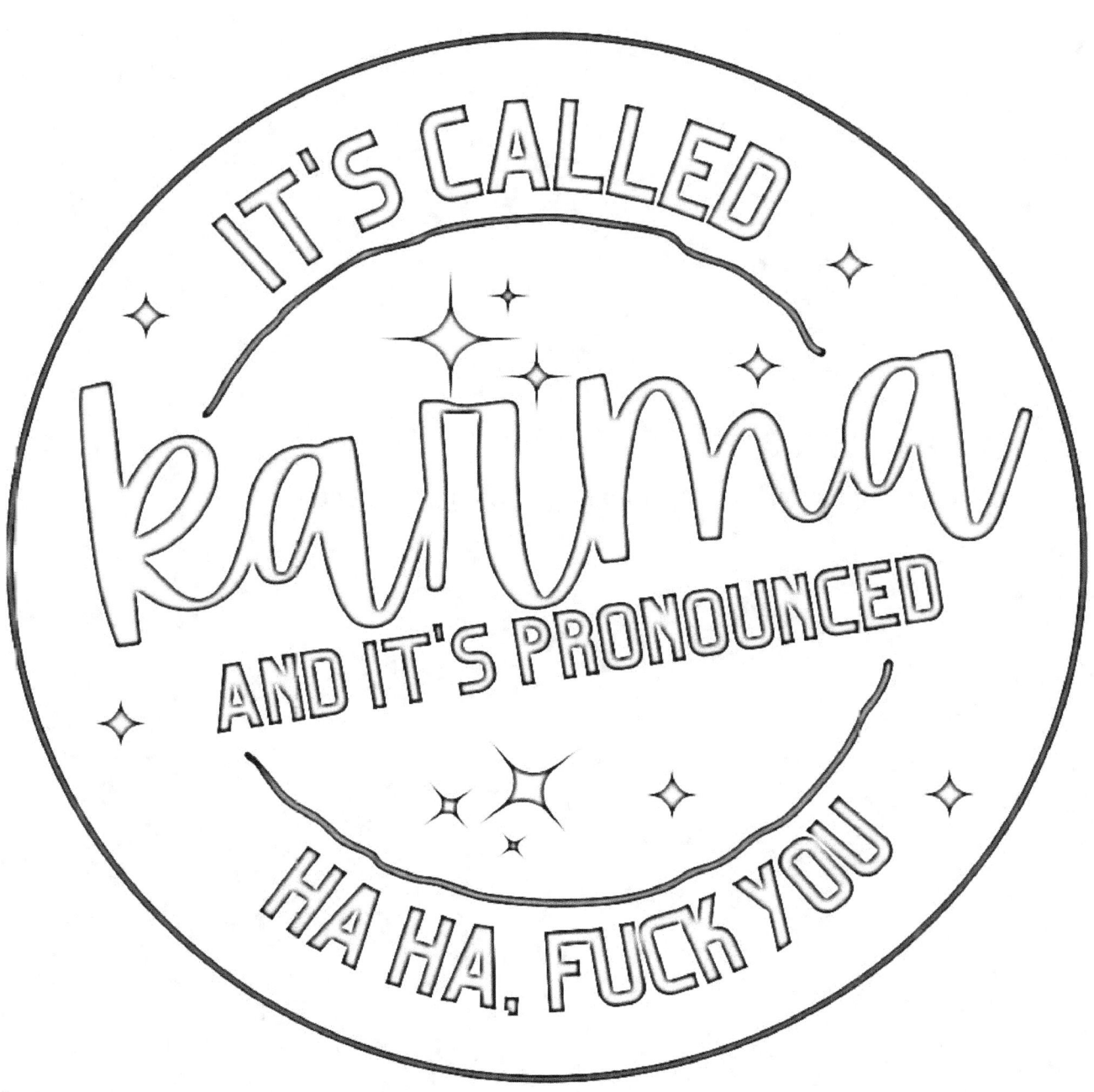

www.KRoseAuthor.net

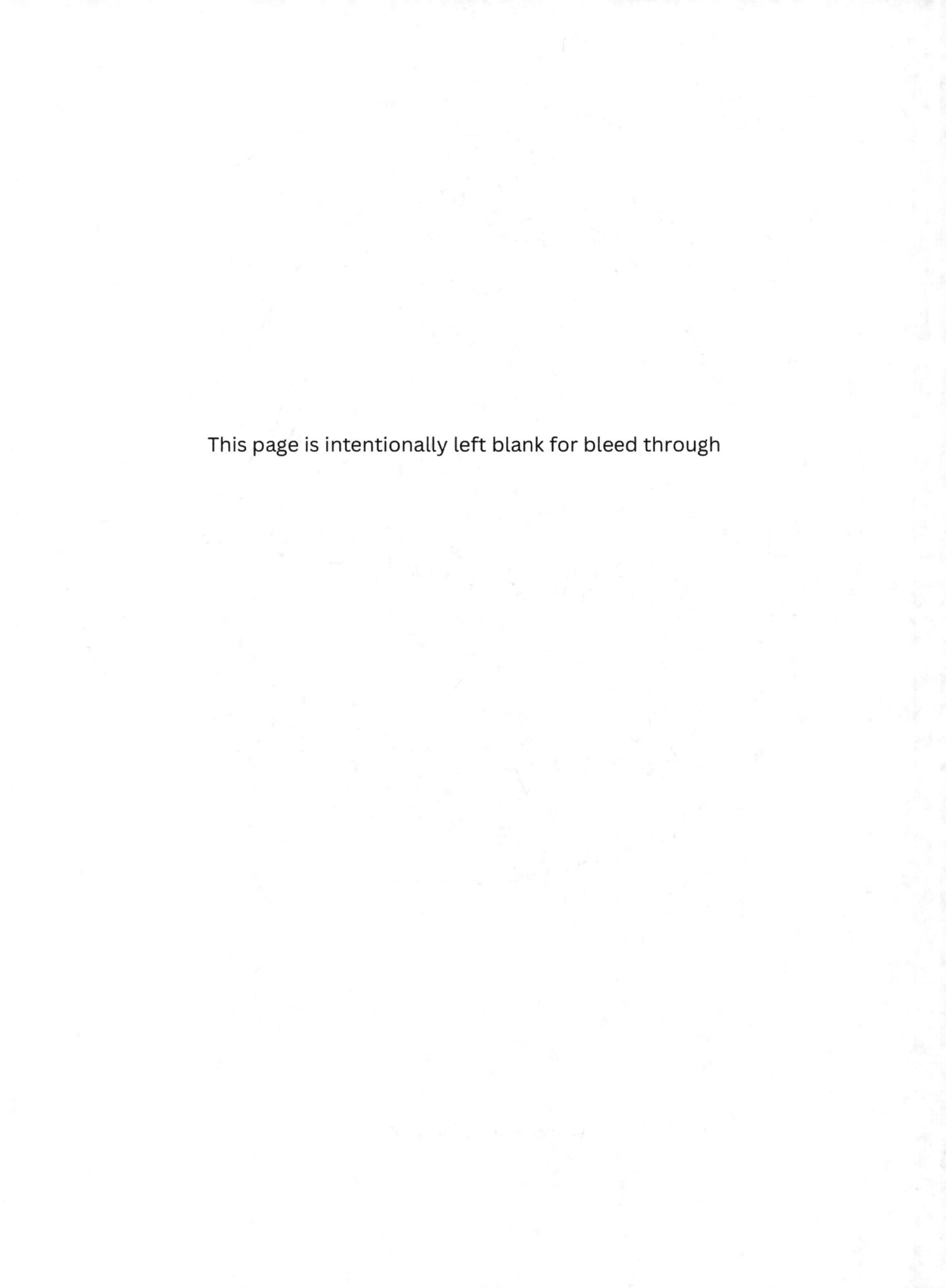

This page is intentionally left blank for bleed through

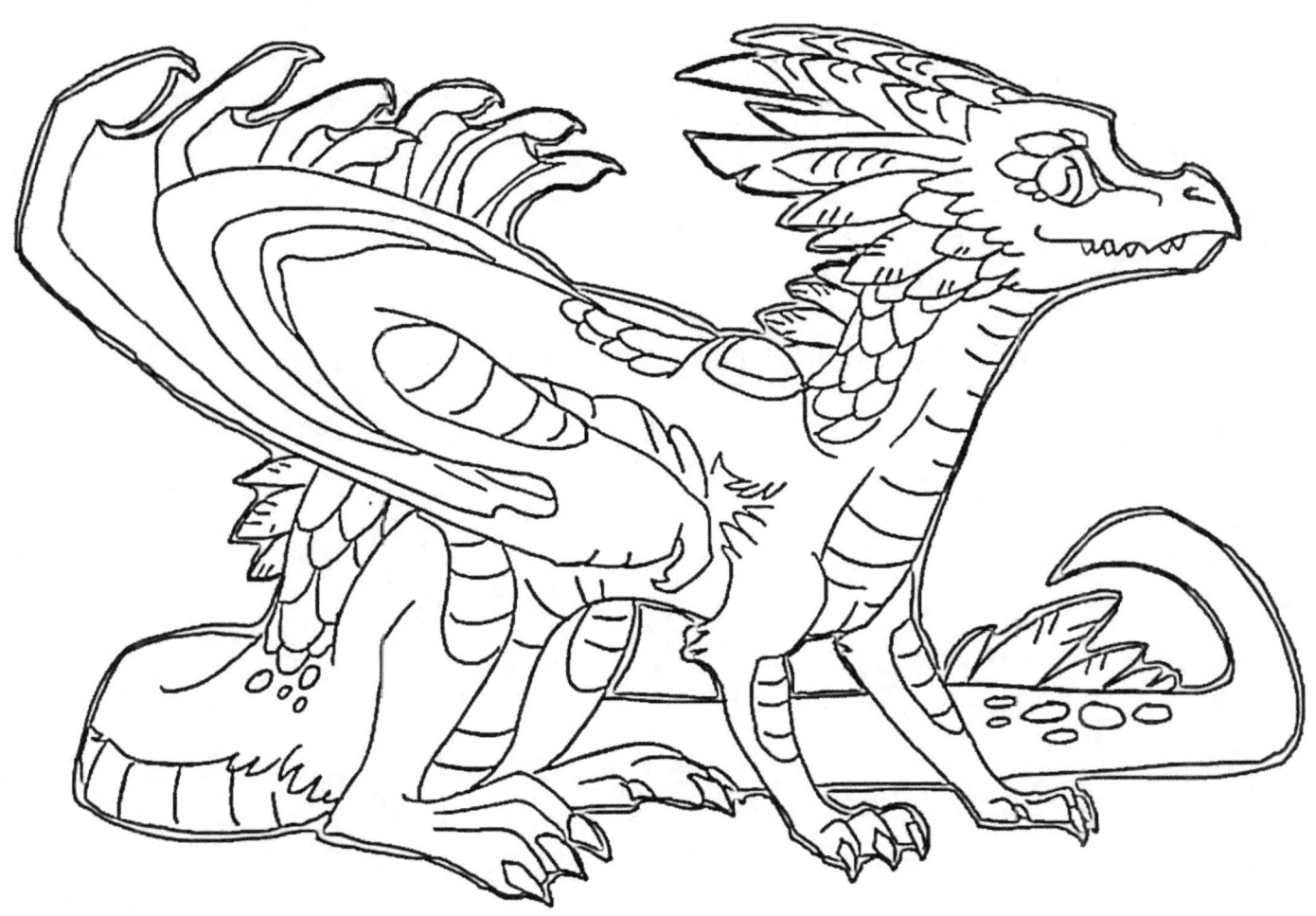

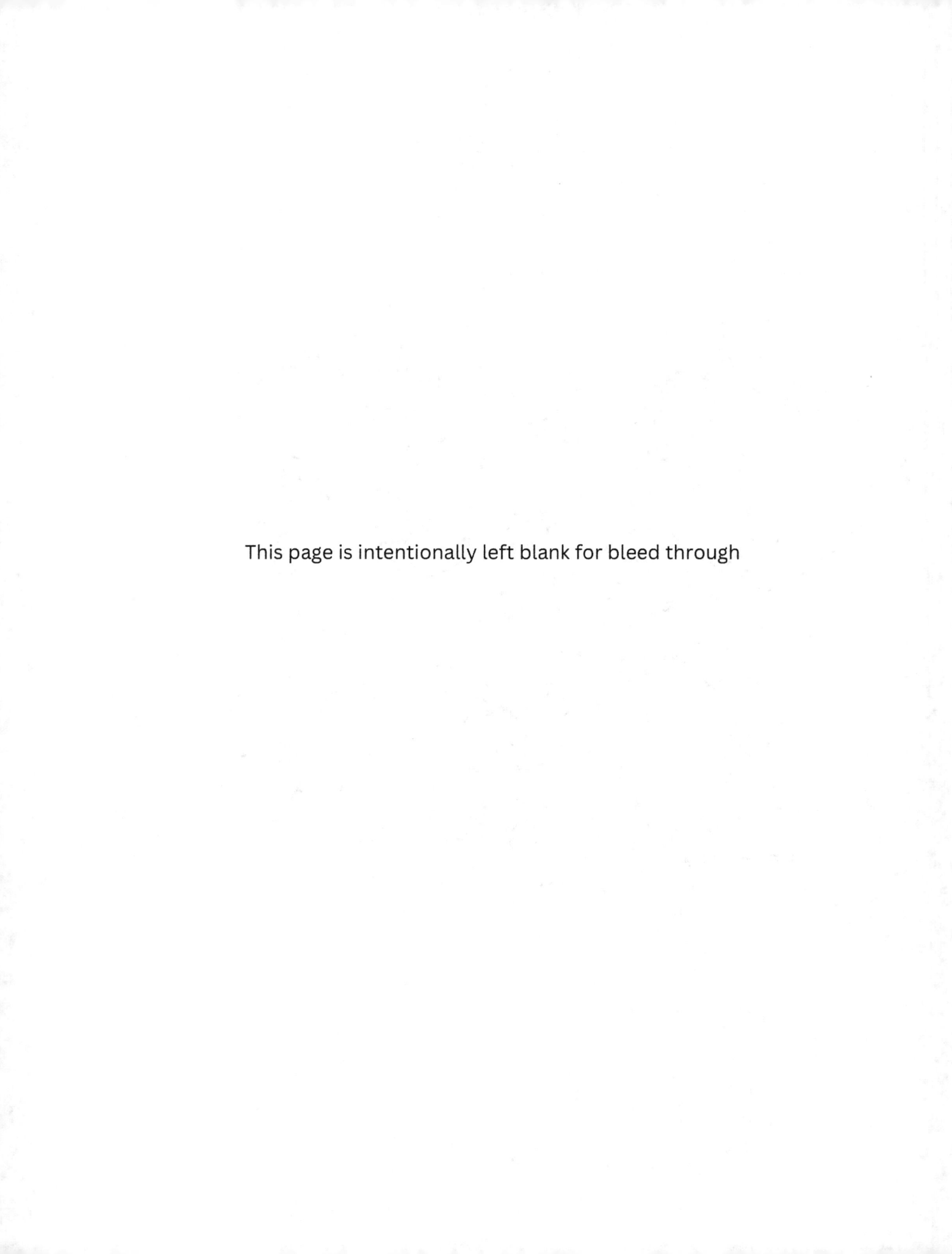

This page is intentionally left blank for bleed through

K. ROSE
INTERNATIONAL BEST SELLING AUTHOR

CHRYSALIS
Club

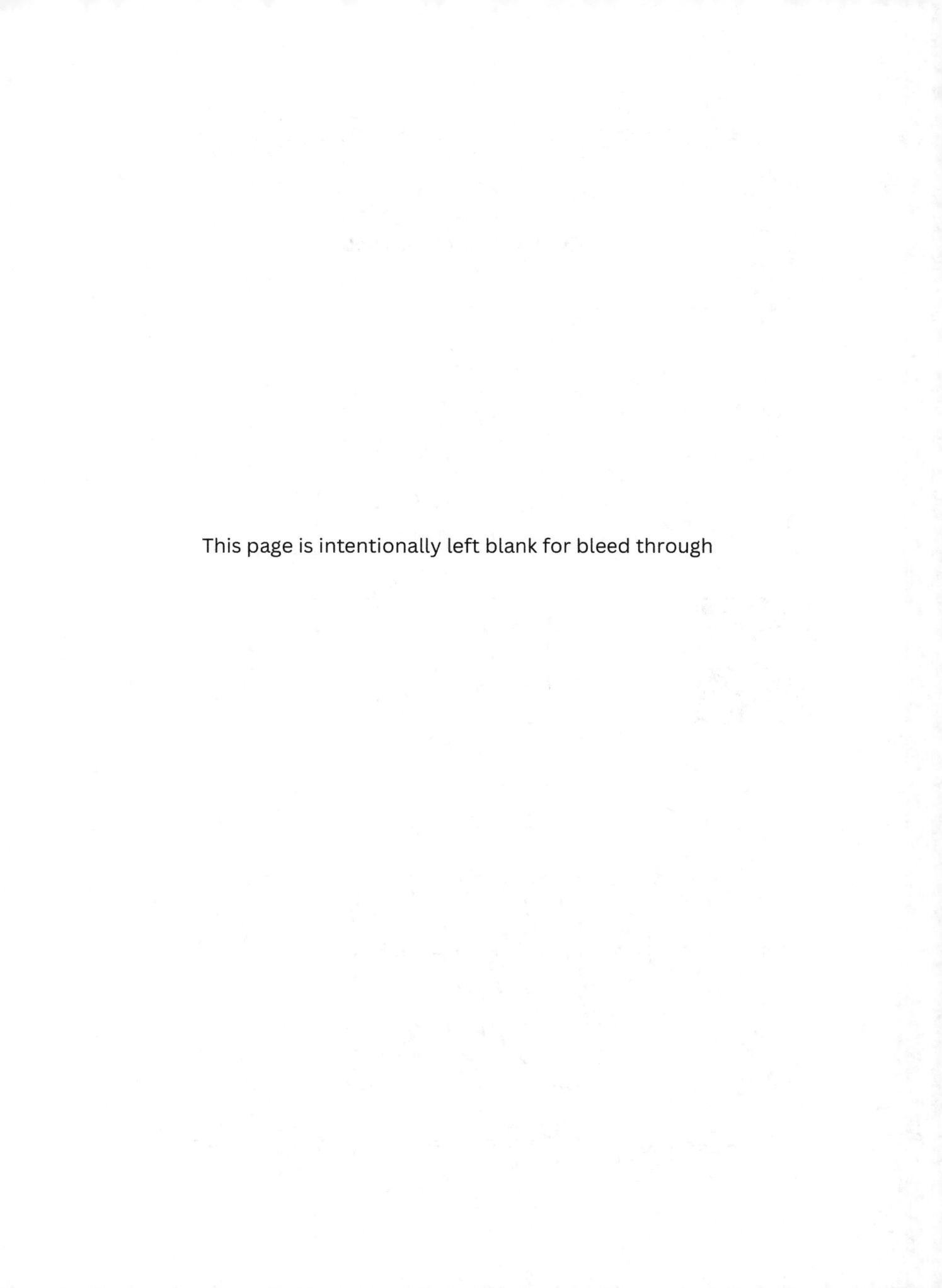

This page is intentionally left blank for bleed through

SYNONYM ROLLS

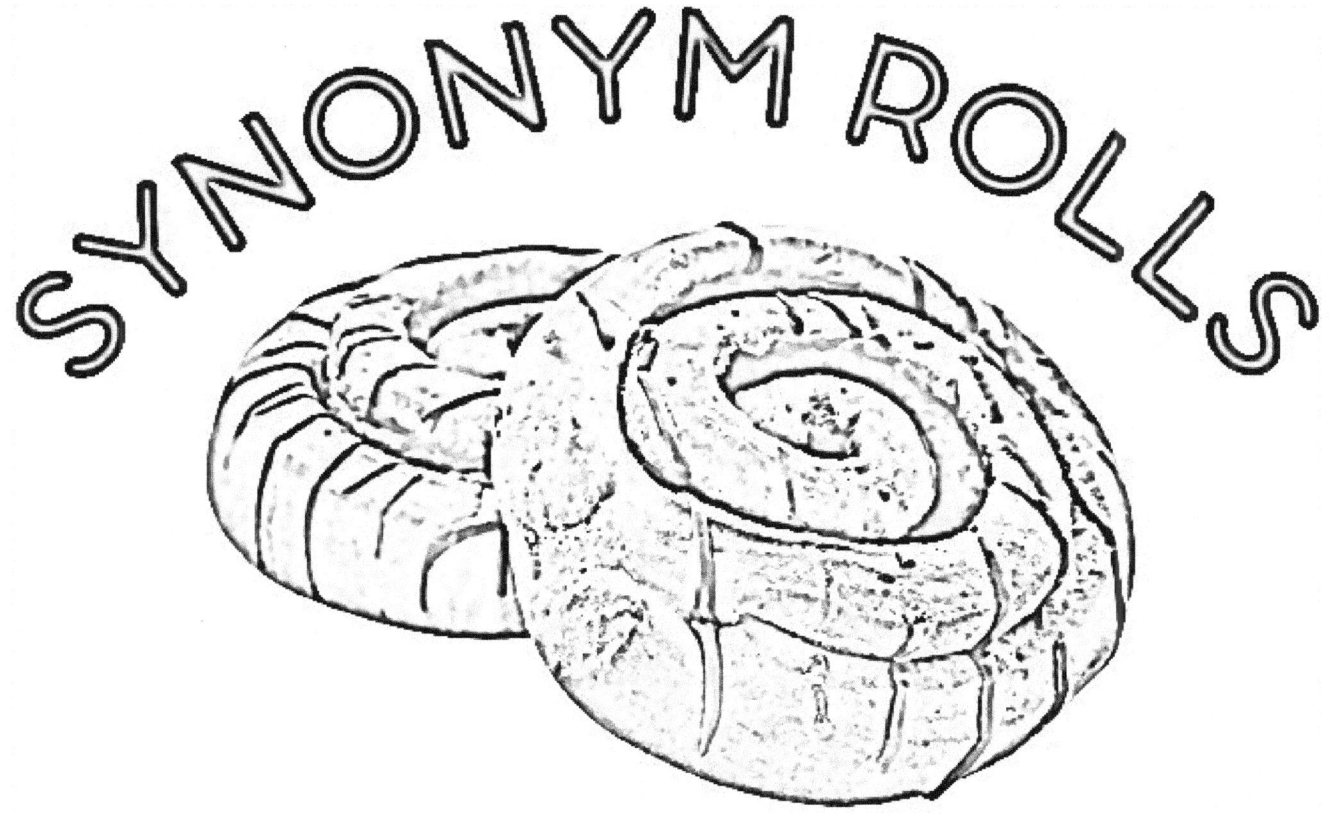

LIKE GRAMMAR

USED TO MAKE

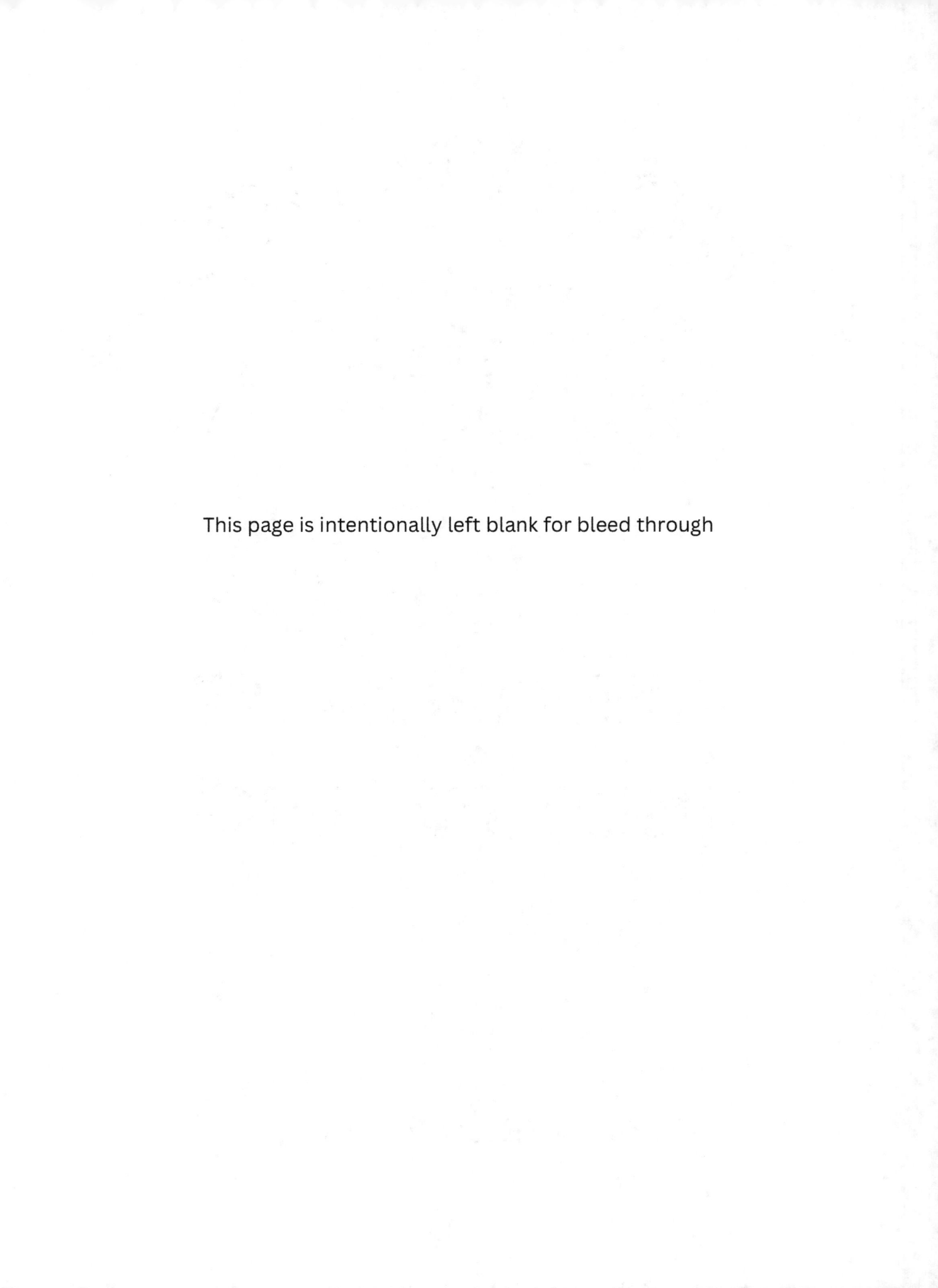

This page is intentionally left blank for bleed through

Lil One - Featured in The Elven Prince

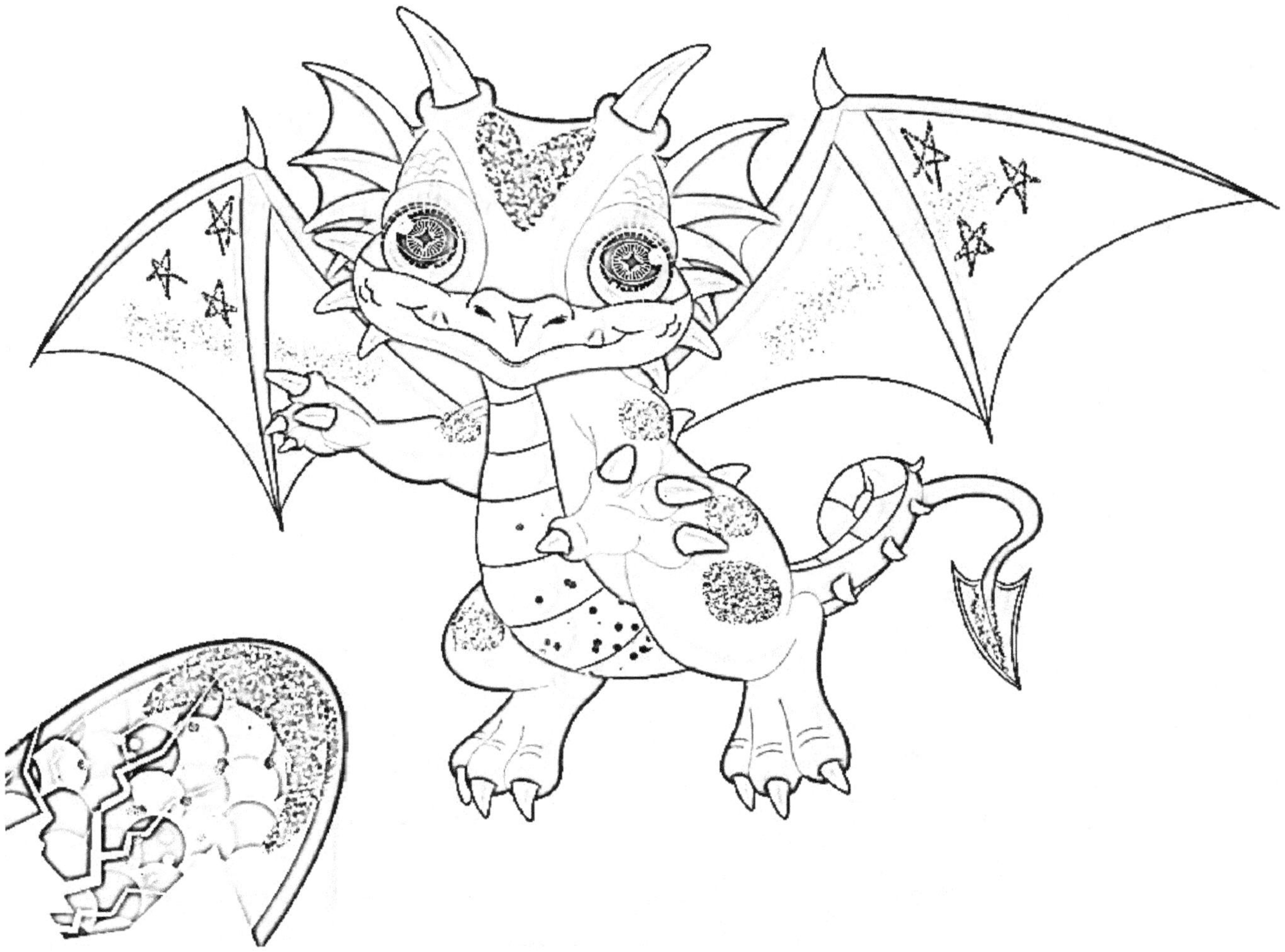

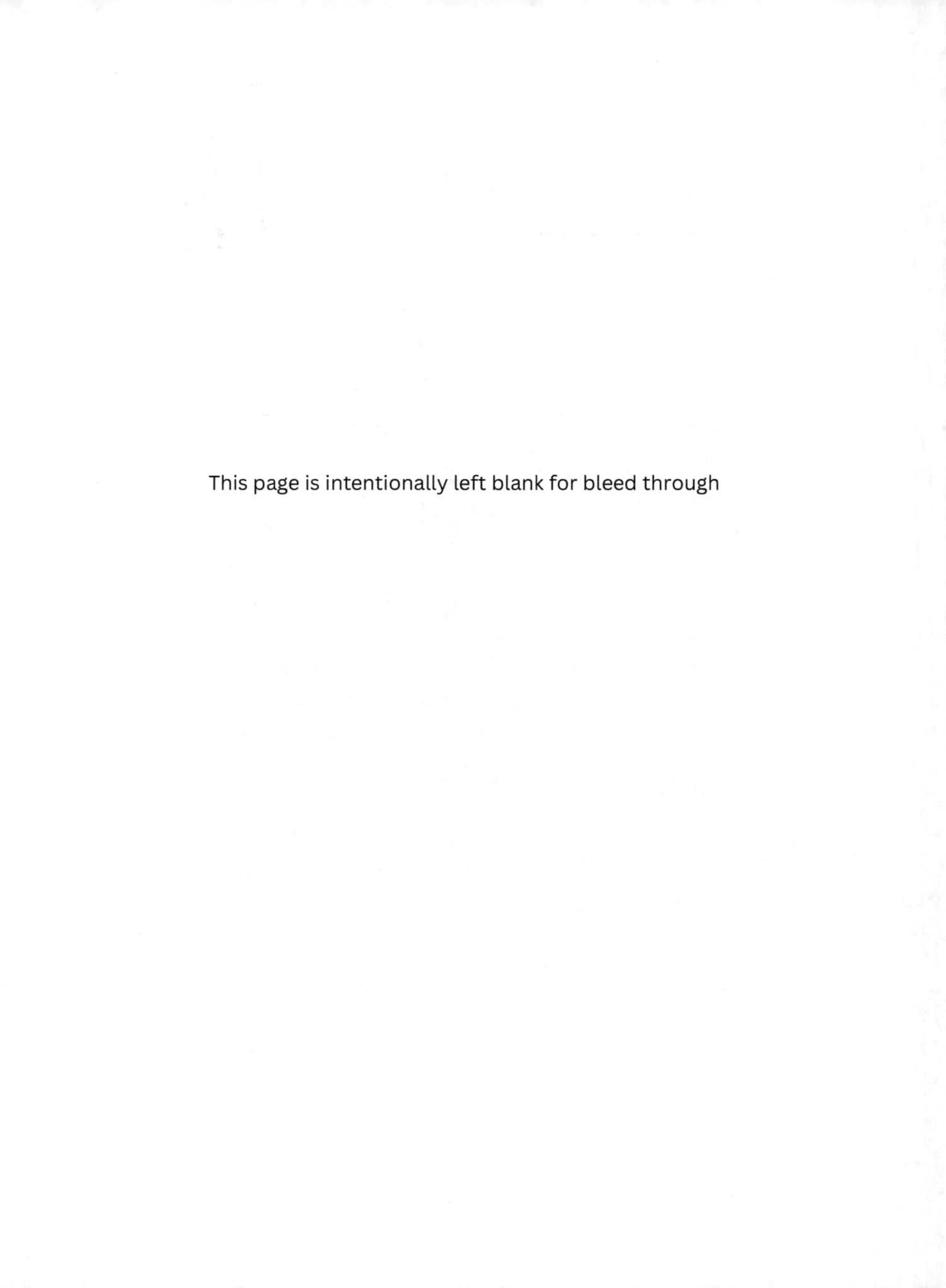

This page is intentionally left blank for bleed through

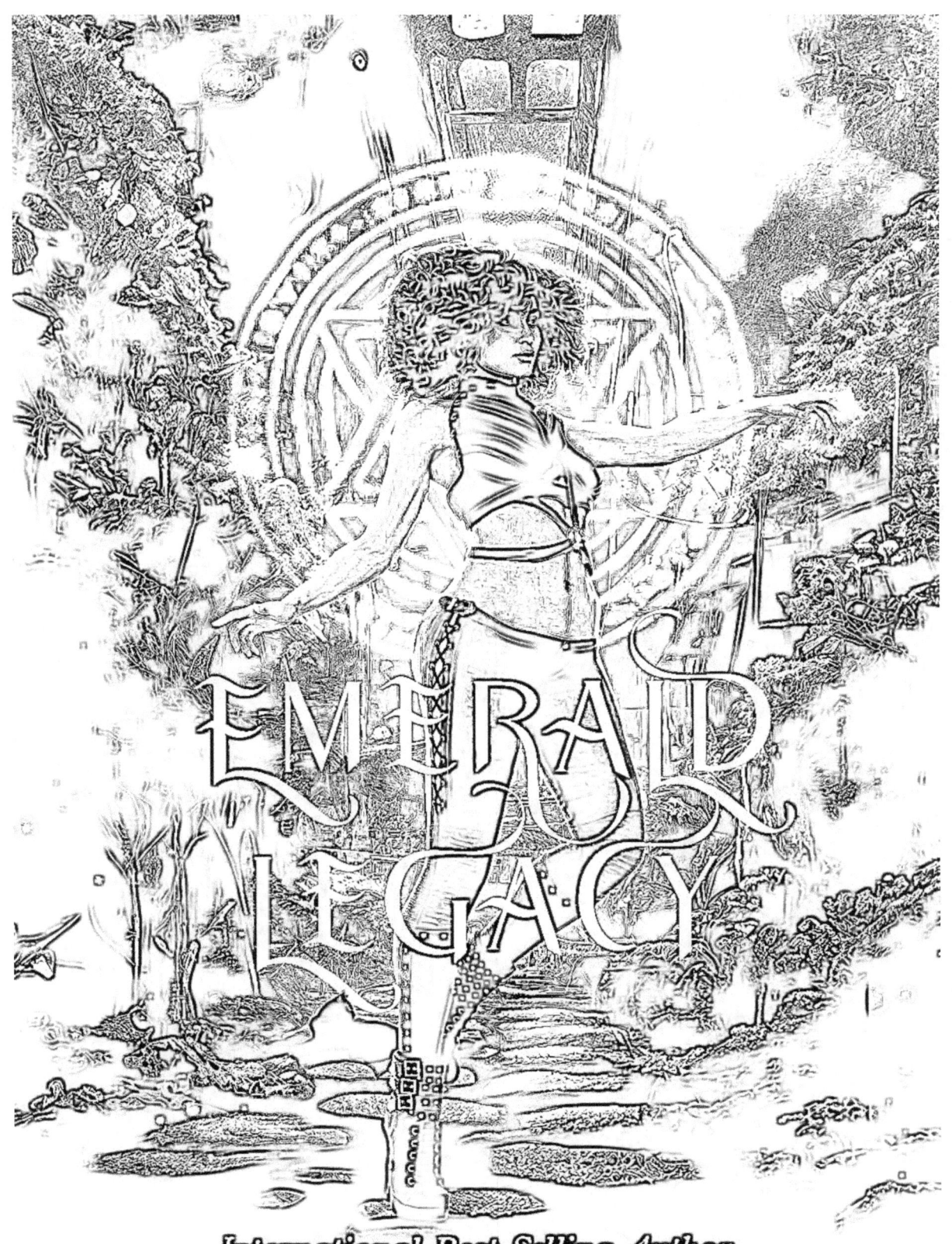

EMERALD LEGACY

International Best Selling Author
K. ROSE

This page is intentionally left blank for bleed through

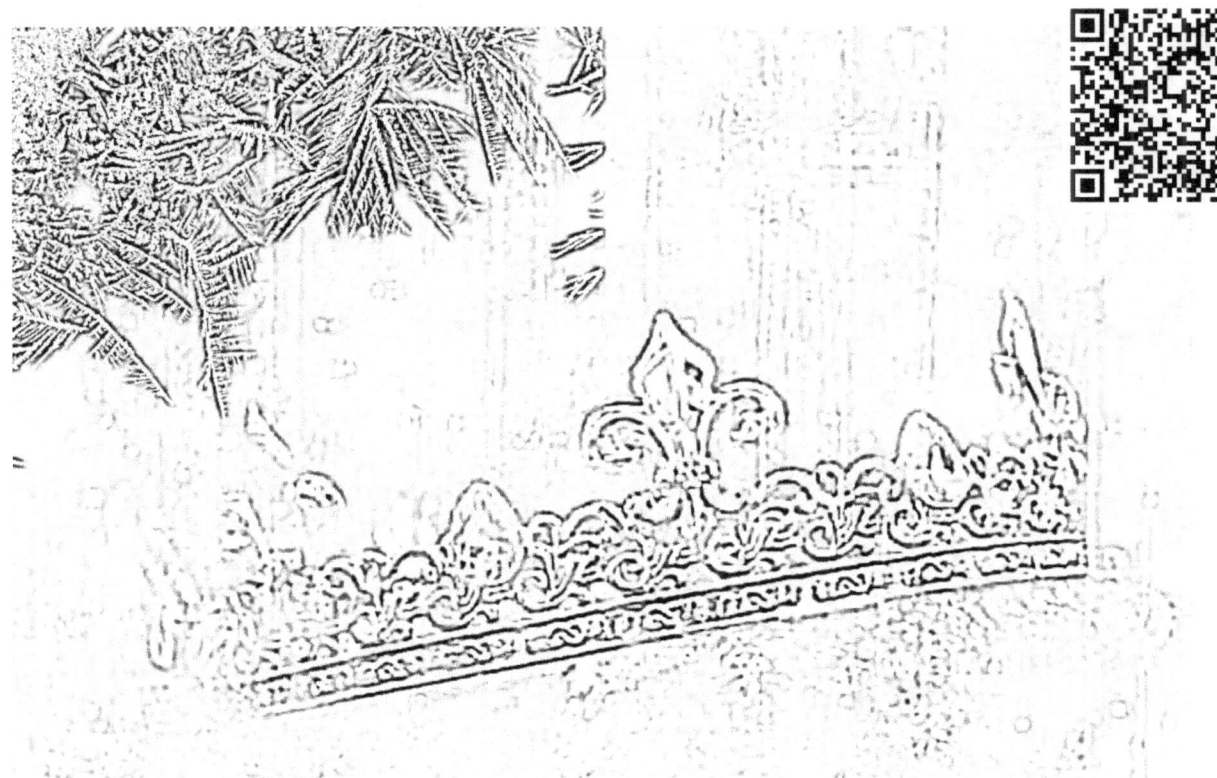

Bound
To The
Fae

International Best Selling Author

K. Rose

This page is intentionally left blank for bleed through

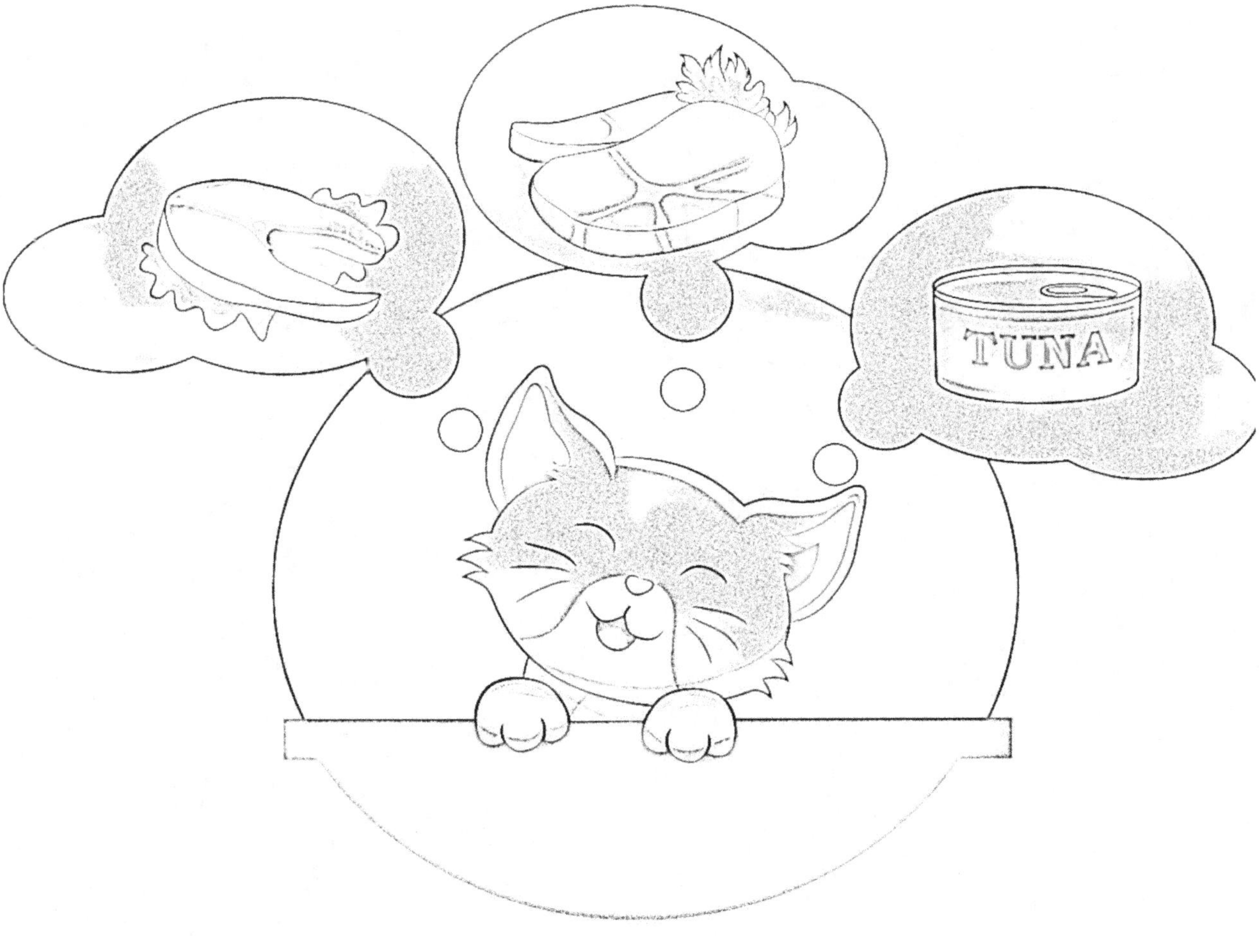

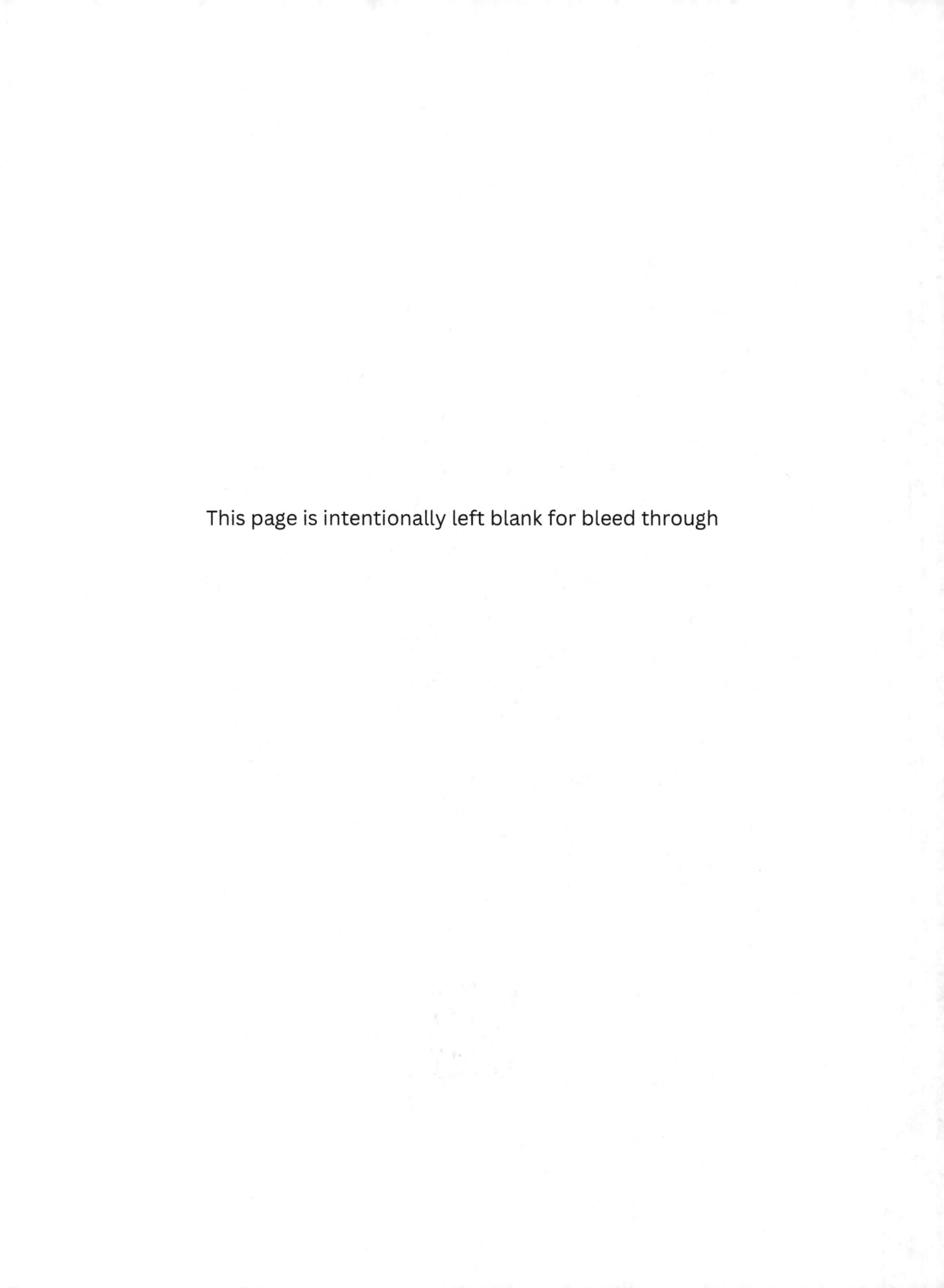

This page is intentionally left blank for bleed through

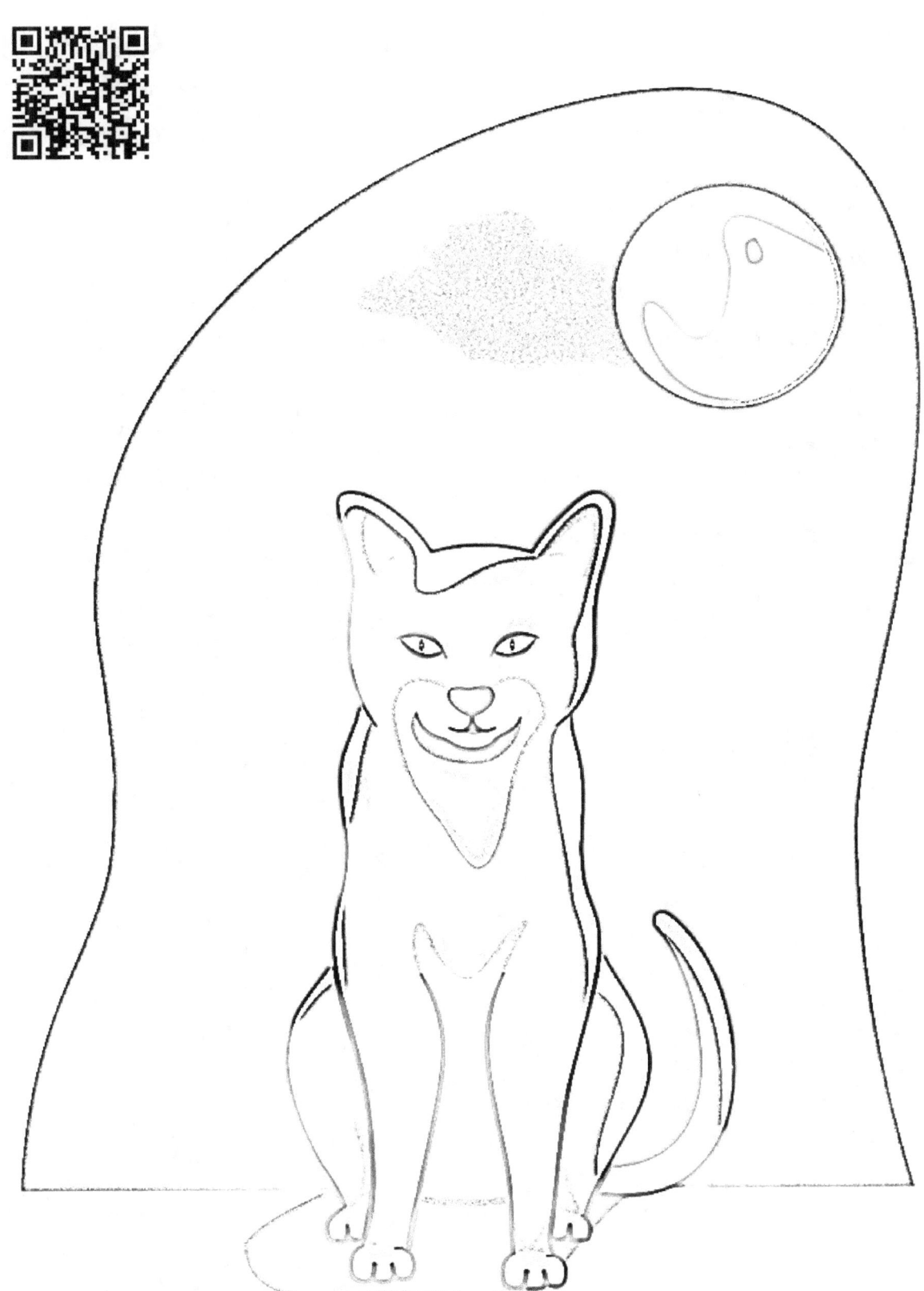

This page is intentionally left blank for bleed through

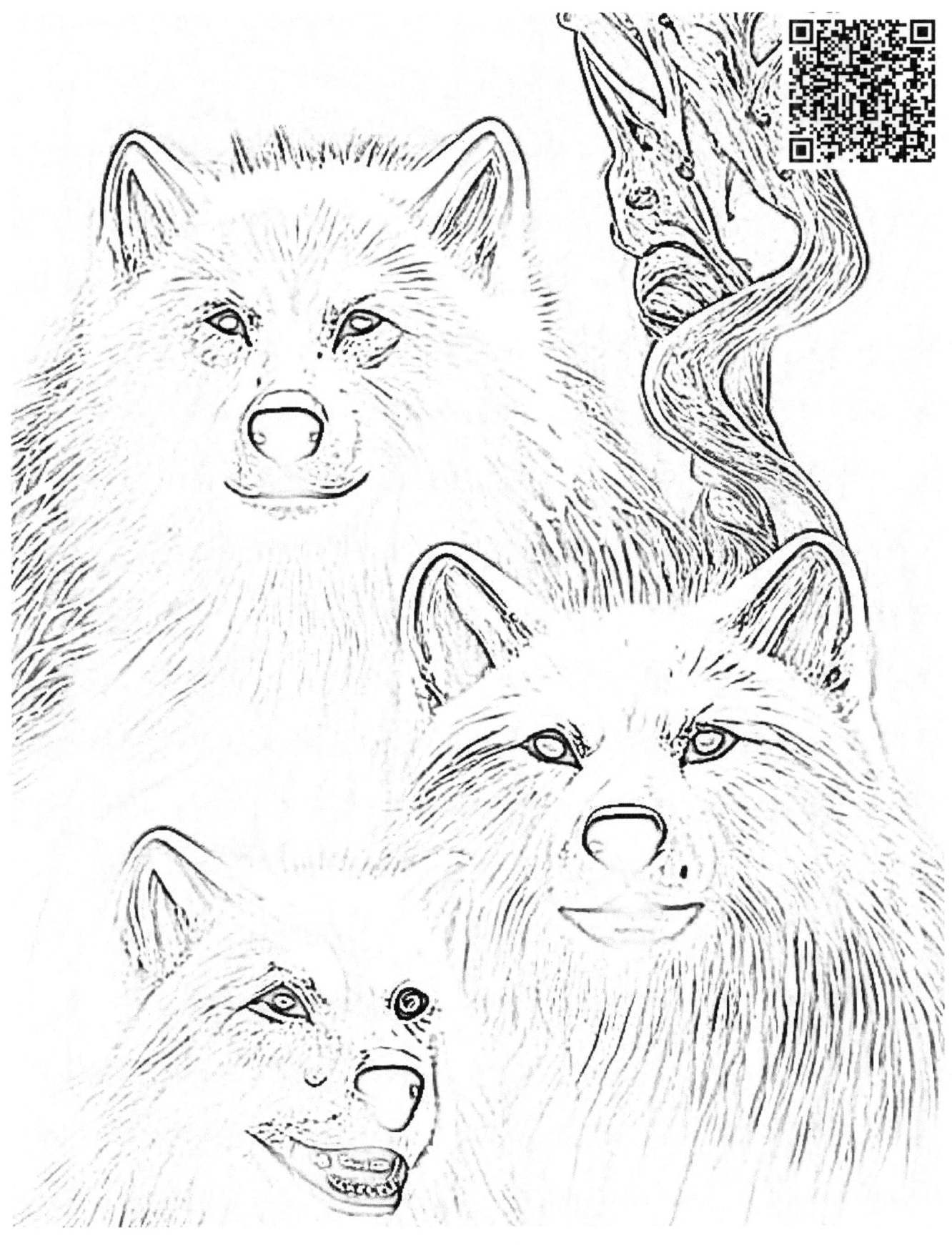

This page is intentionally left blank for bleed through

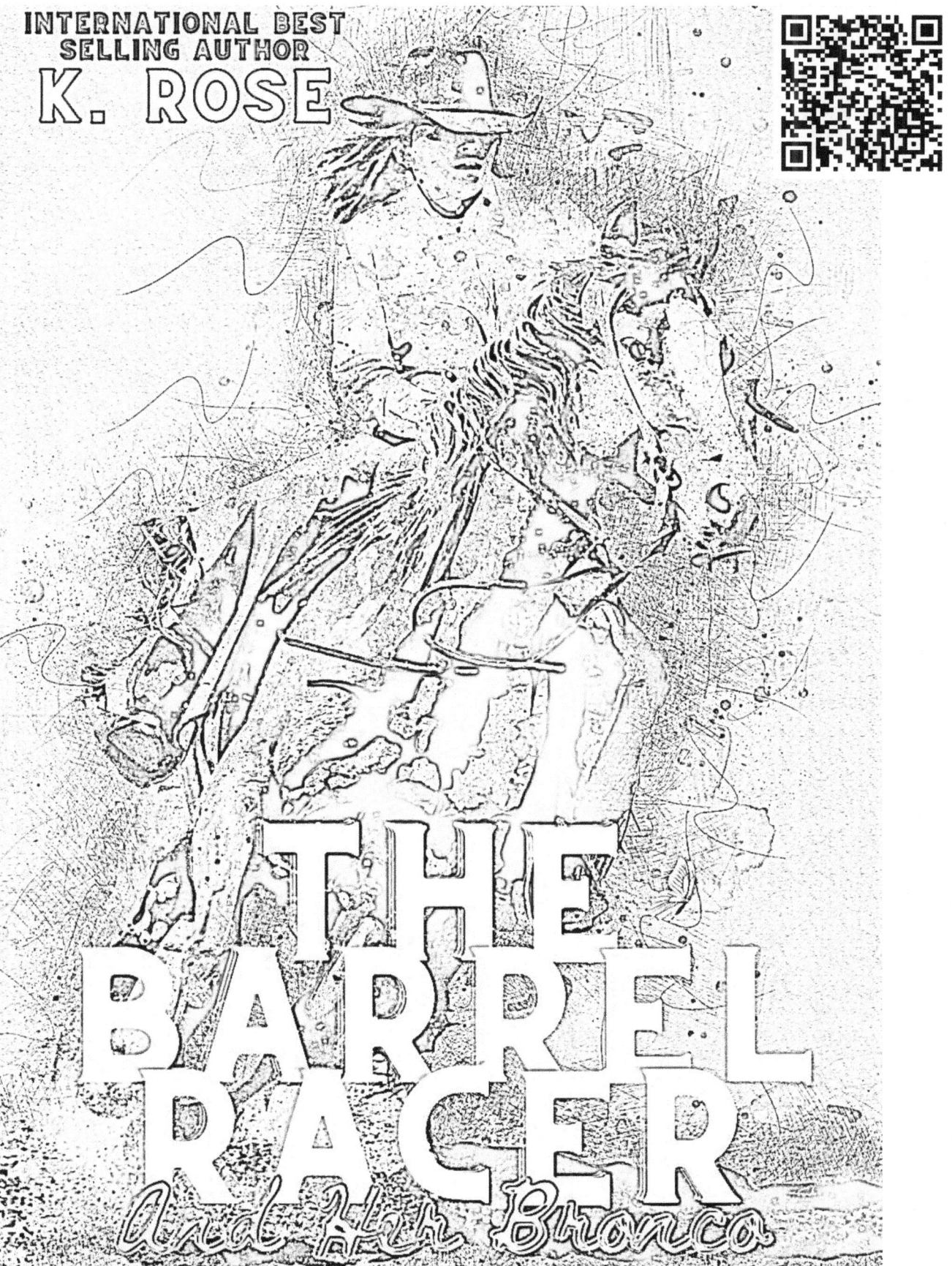

INTERNATIONAL BEST
SELLING AUTHOR
K. ROSE

THE
BARREL
RACER
And Her Bronco

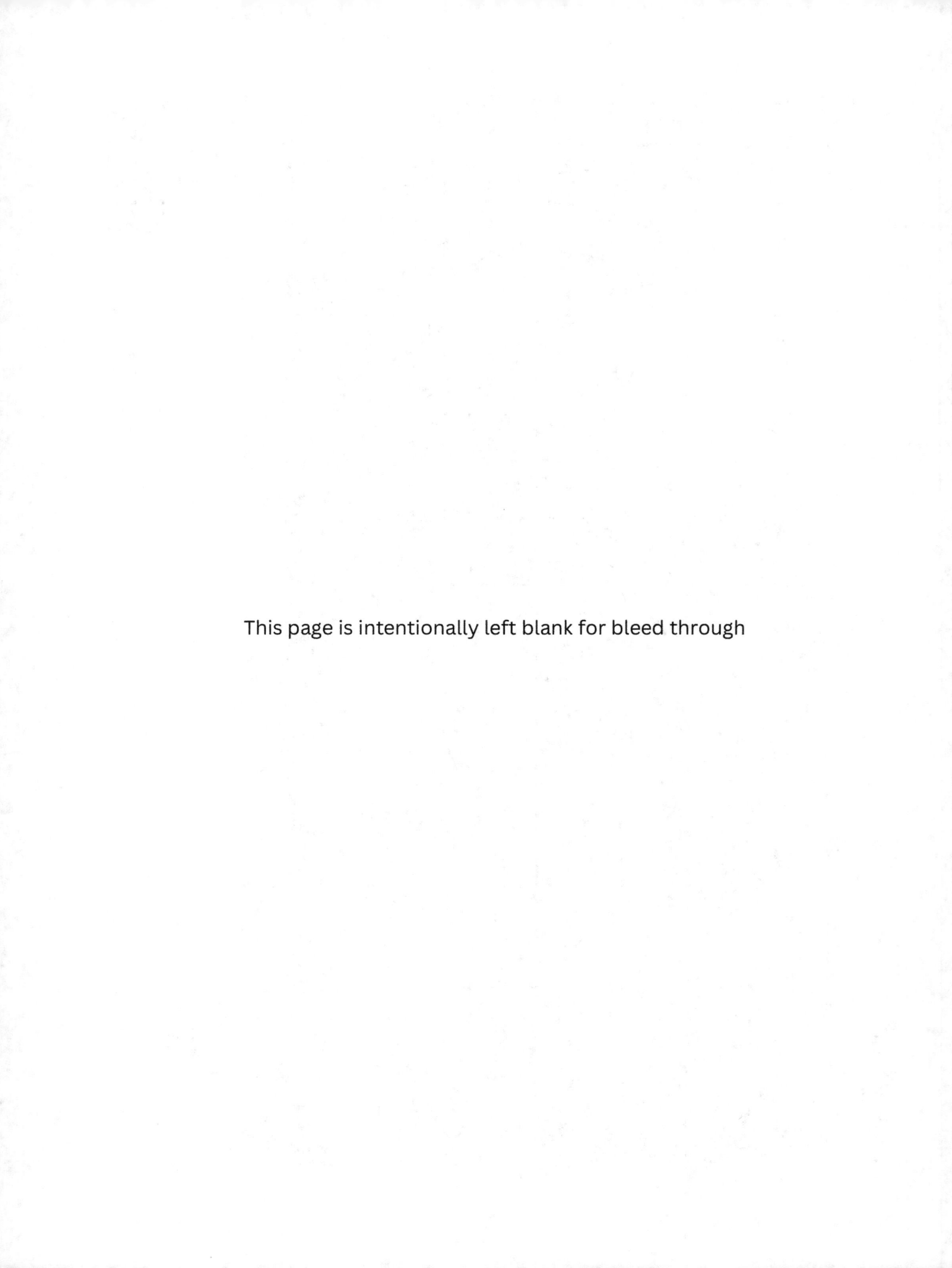

This page is intentionally left blank for bleed through

Vale

The Prophecy of the Water Sprite

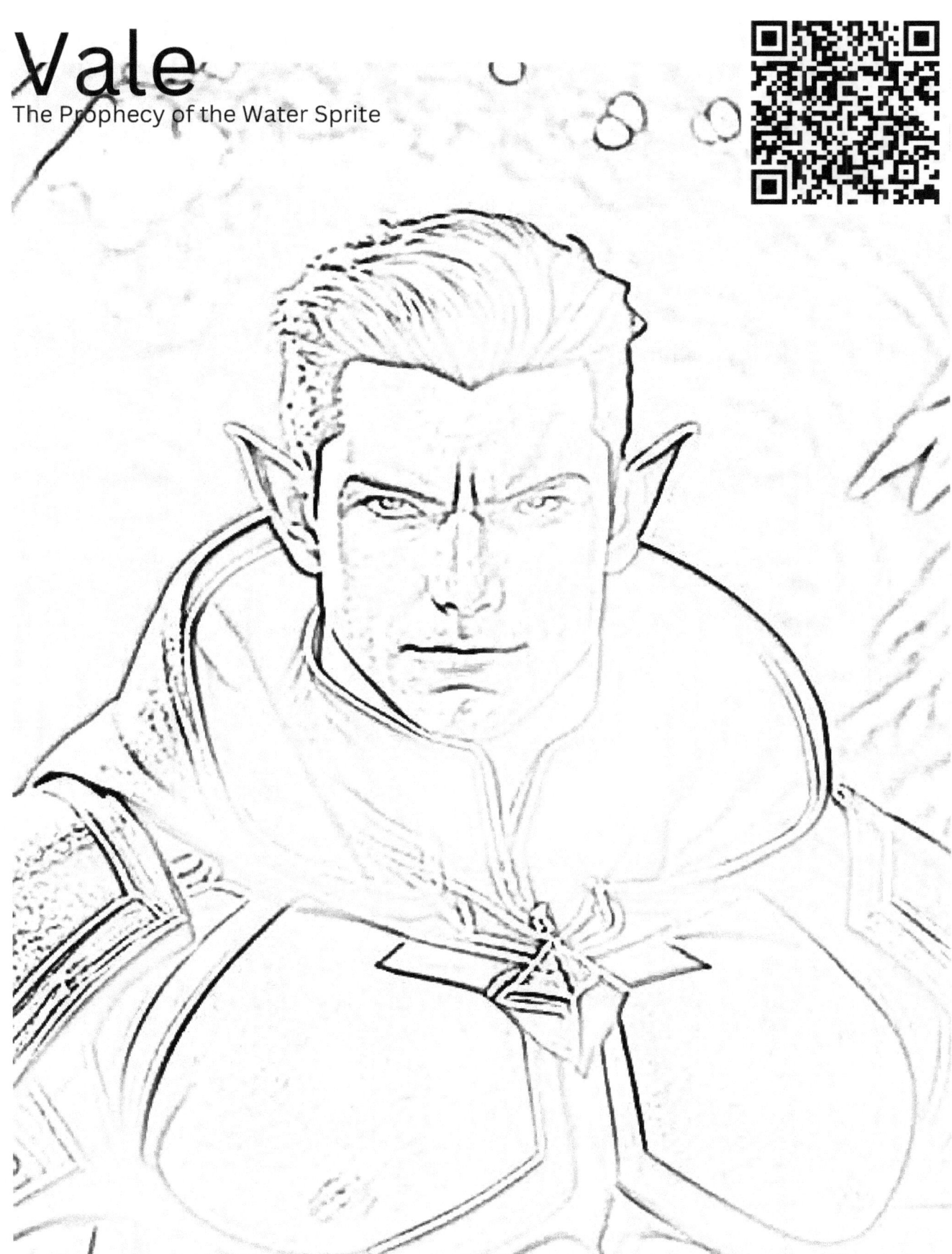

This page is intentionally left blank for bleed through

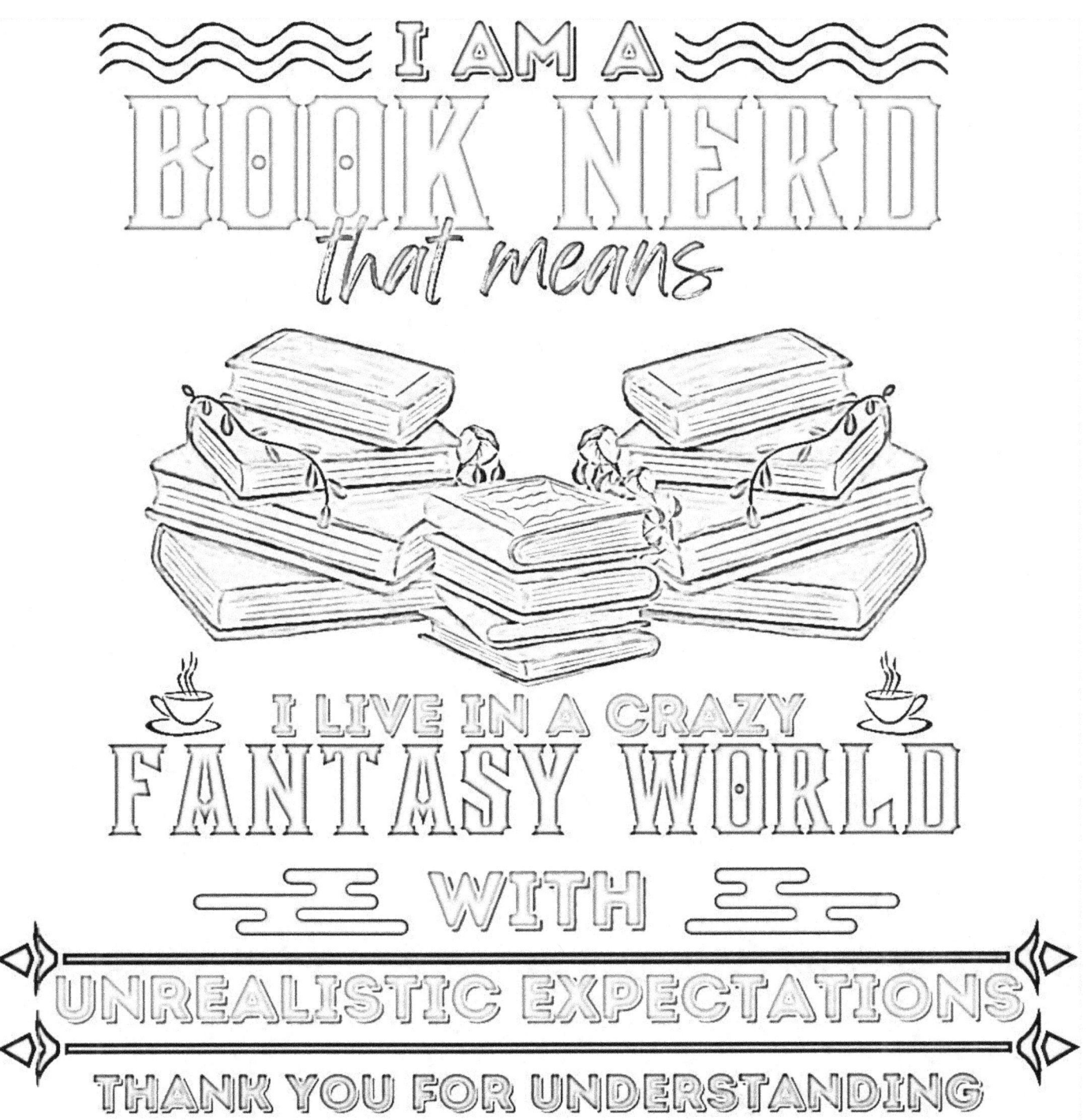

I AM A
BOOK NERD
that means

I LIVE IN A CRAZY
FANTASY WORLD
WITH

UNREALISTIC EXPECTATIONS

THANK YOU FOR UNDERSTANDING

www.KRoseAuthor.net

This page is intentionally left blank for bleed through

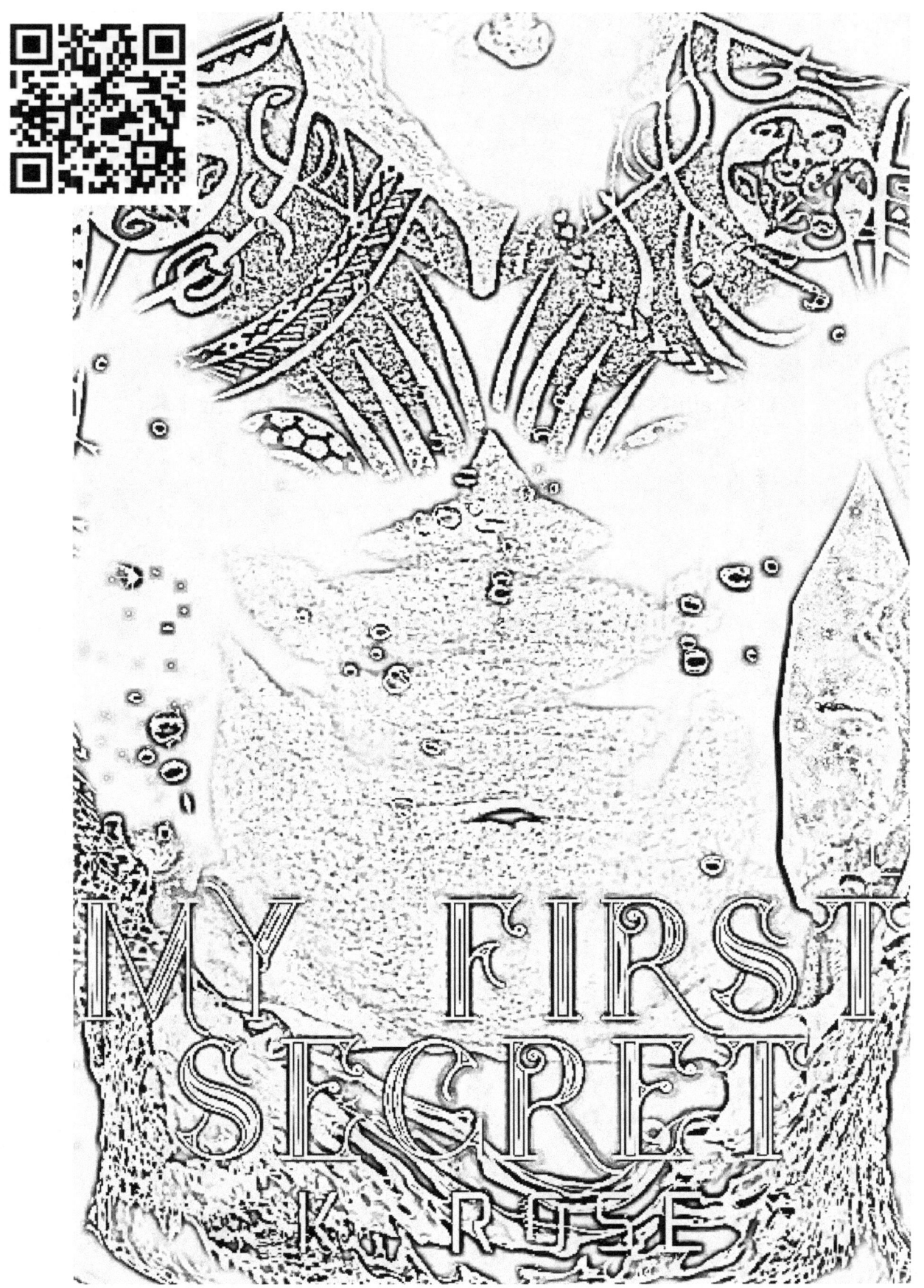

MY FIRST
SECRET
K. ROSE

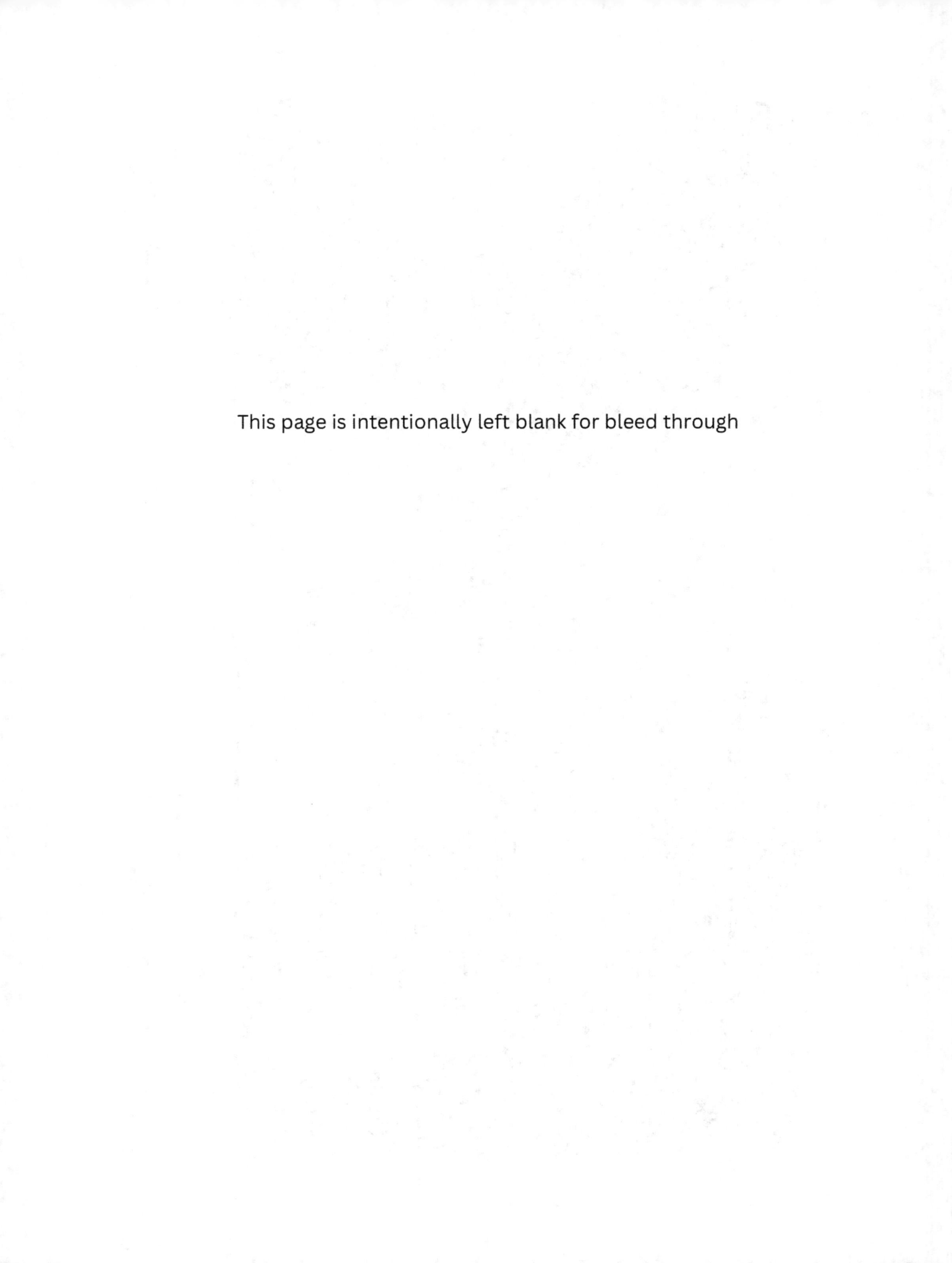

This page is intentionally left blank for bleed through

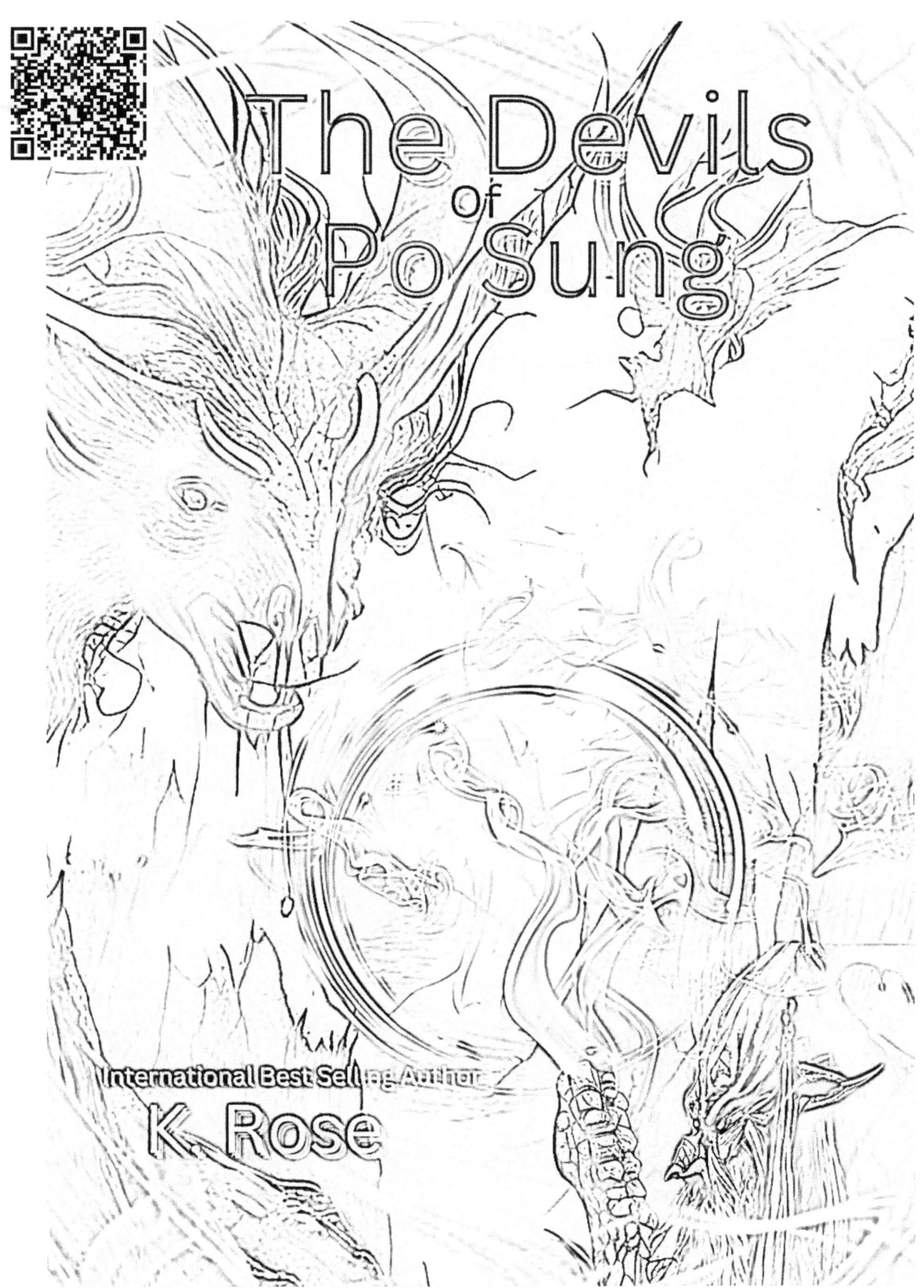

The Devils of Po Sung

International Best Selling Author

K. Rose

This page is intentionally left blank for bleed through

Elio

The Prophecy of the Water Sprite

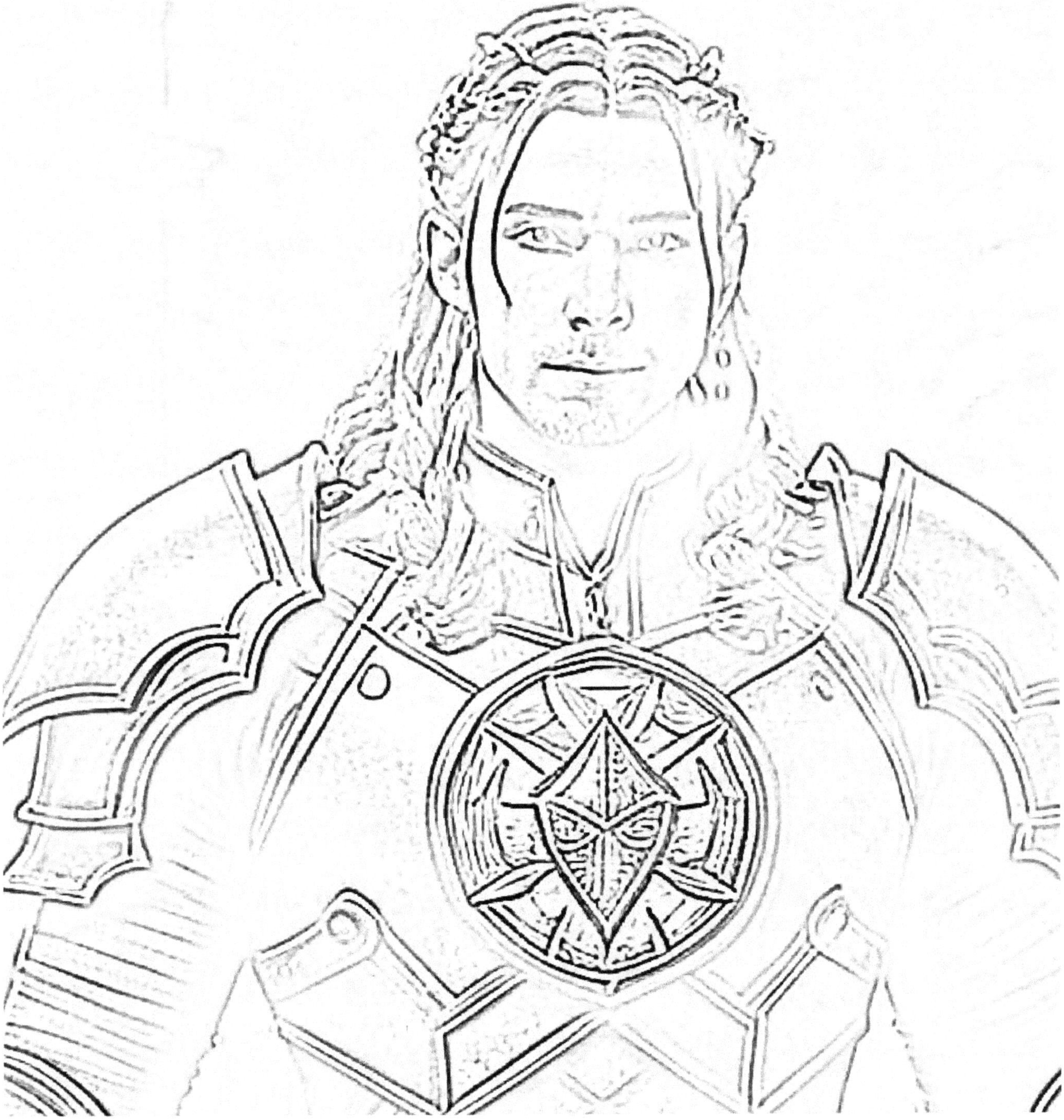

This page is intentionally left blank for bleed through

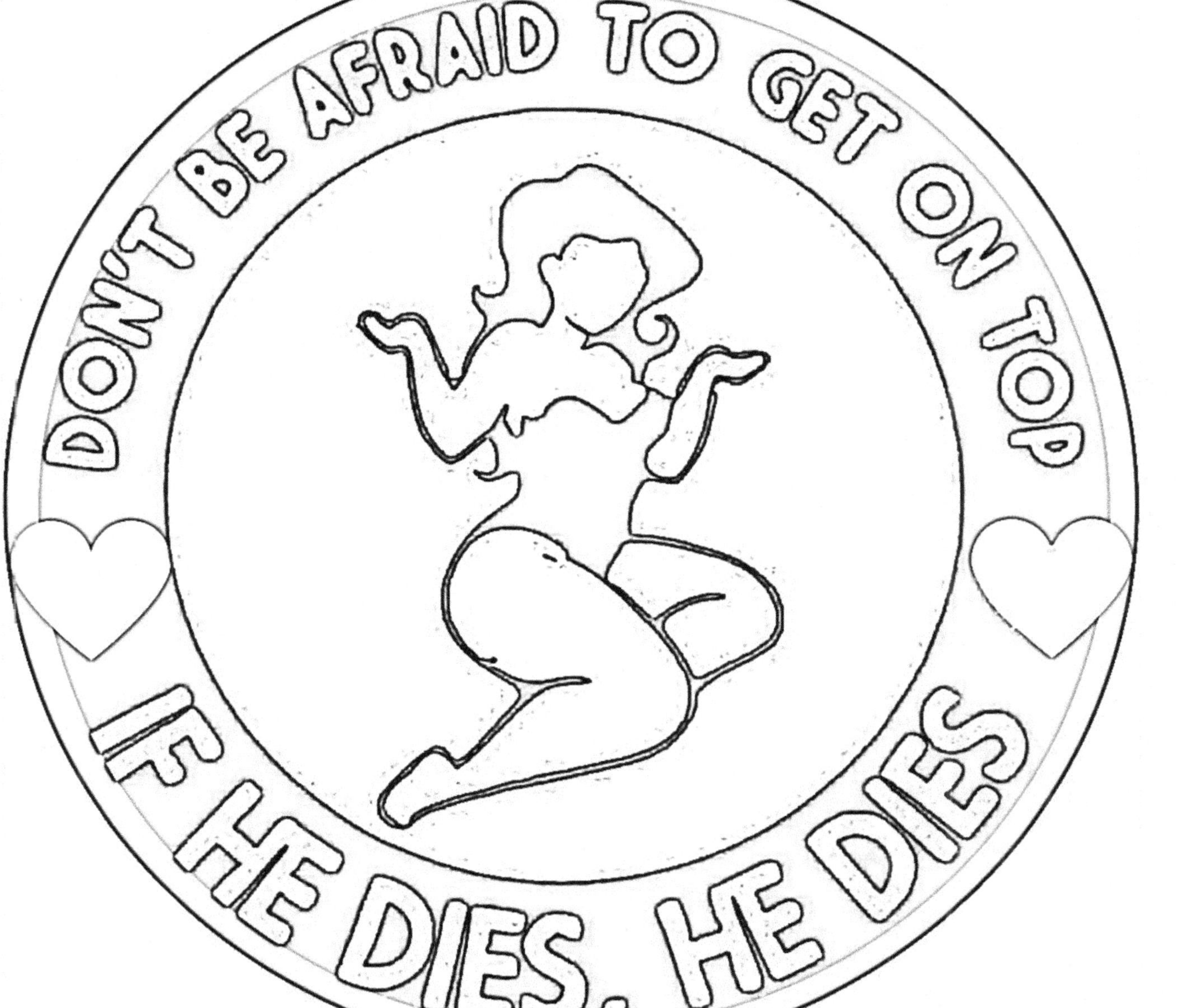

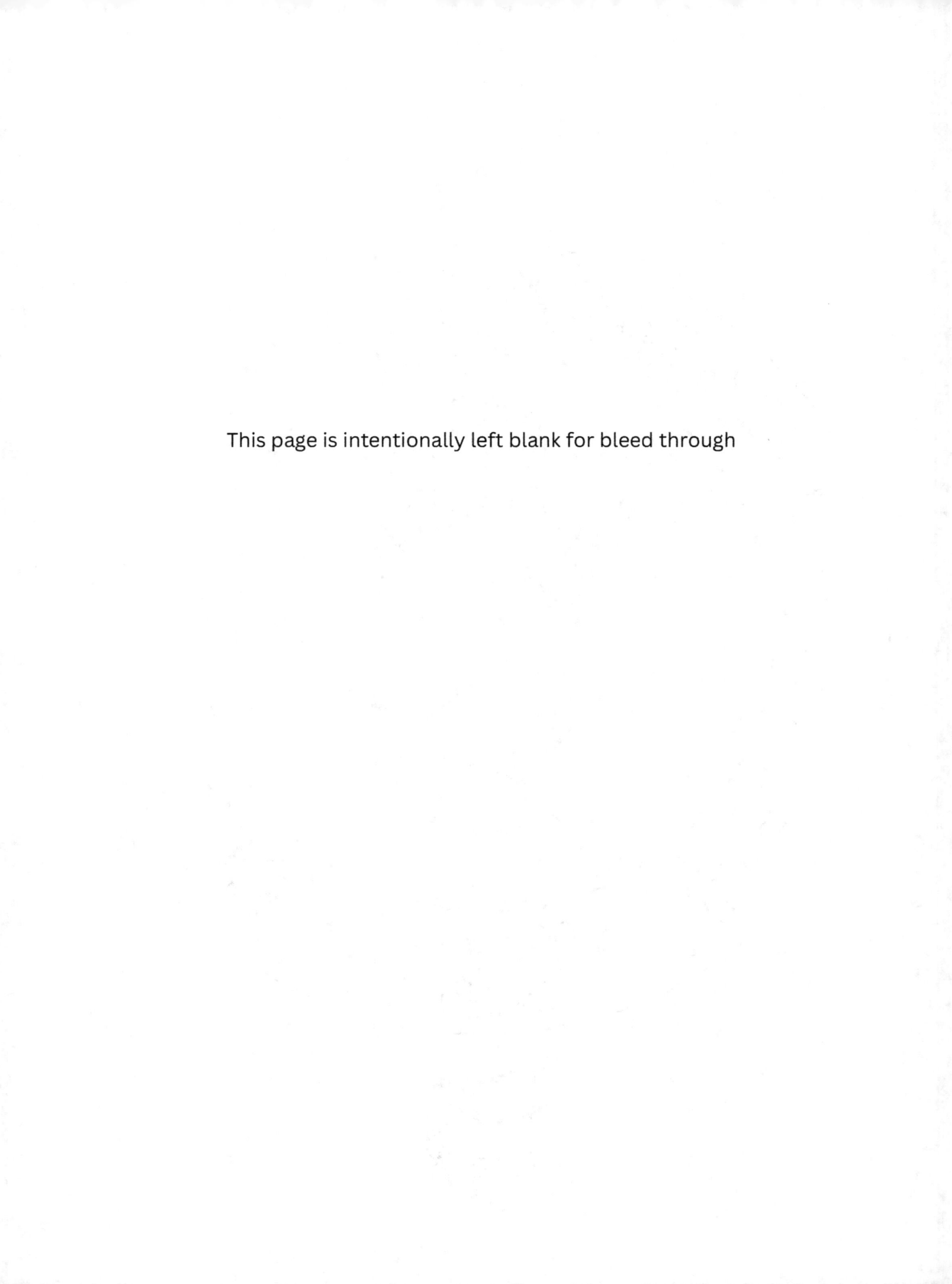

This page is intentionally left blank for bleed through

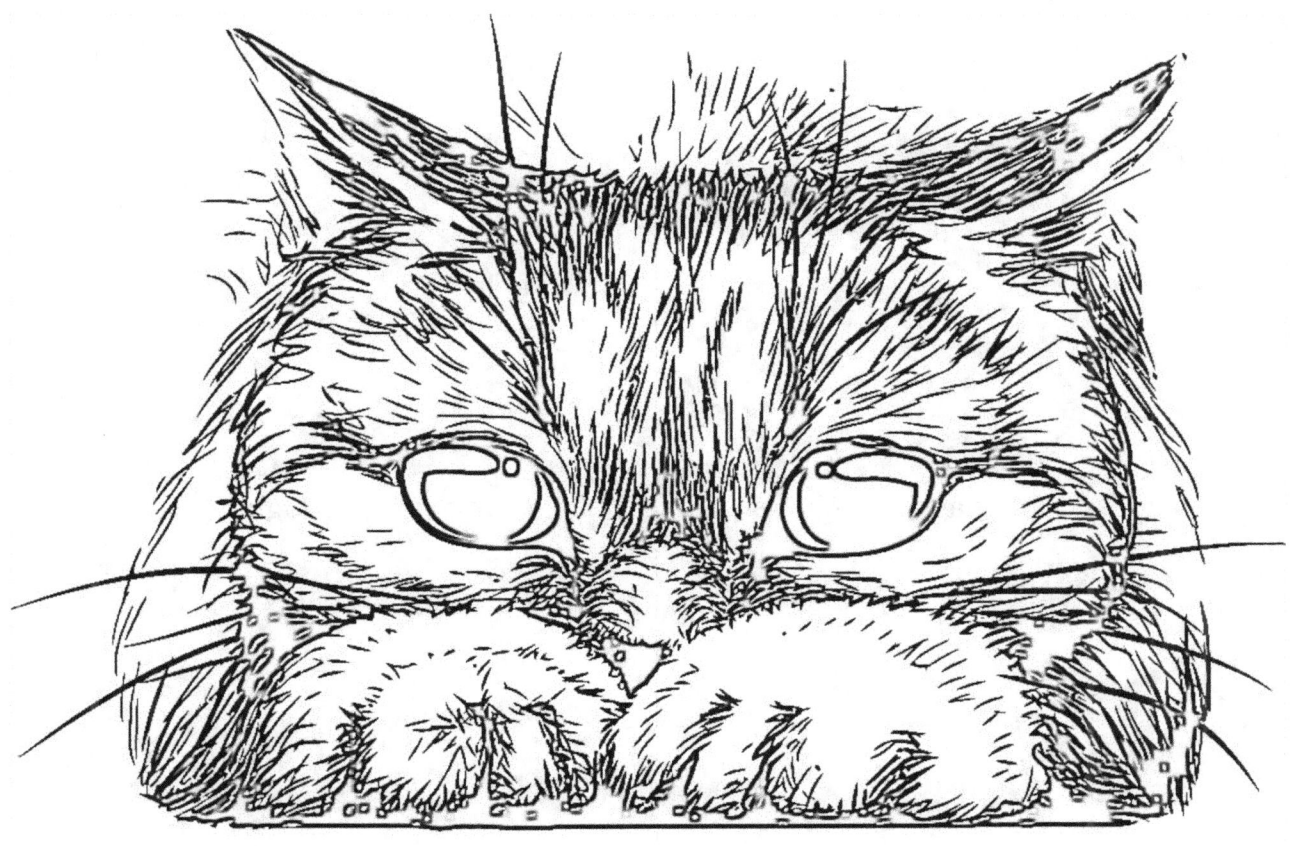

YOU GOTTA BE KITTEN ME

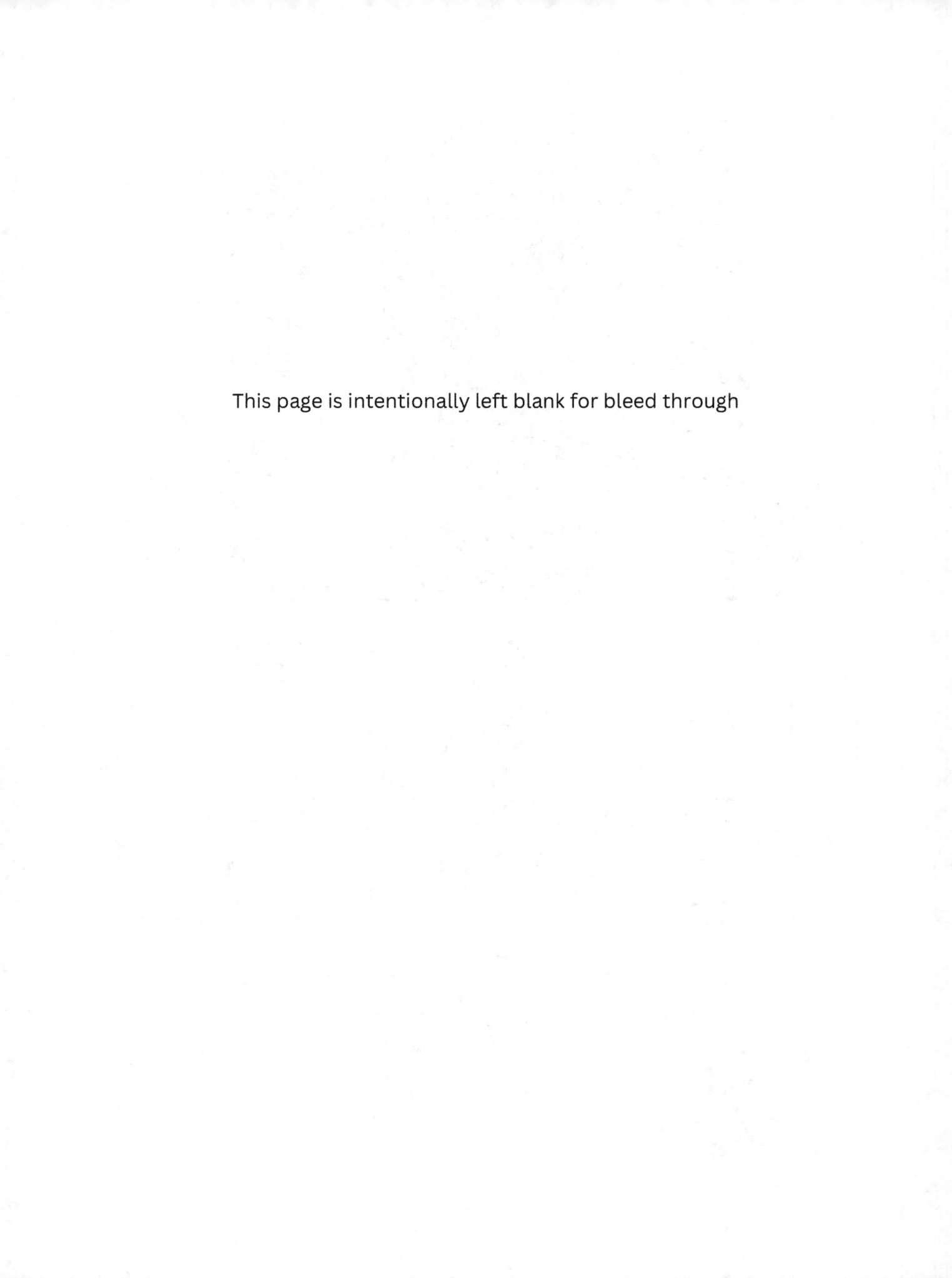

This page is intentionally left blank for bleed through

Freya

Bound to the Fae

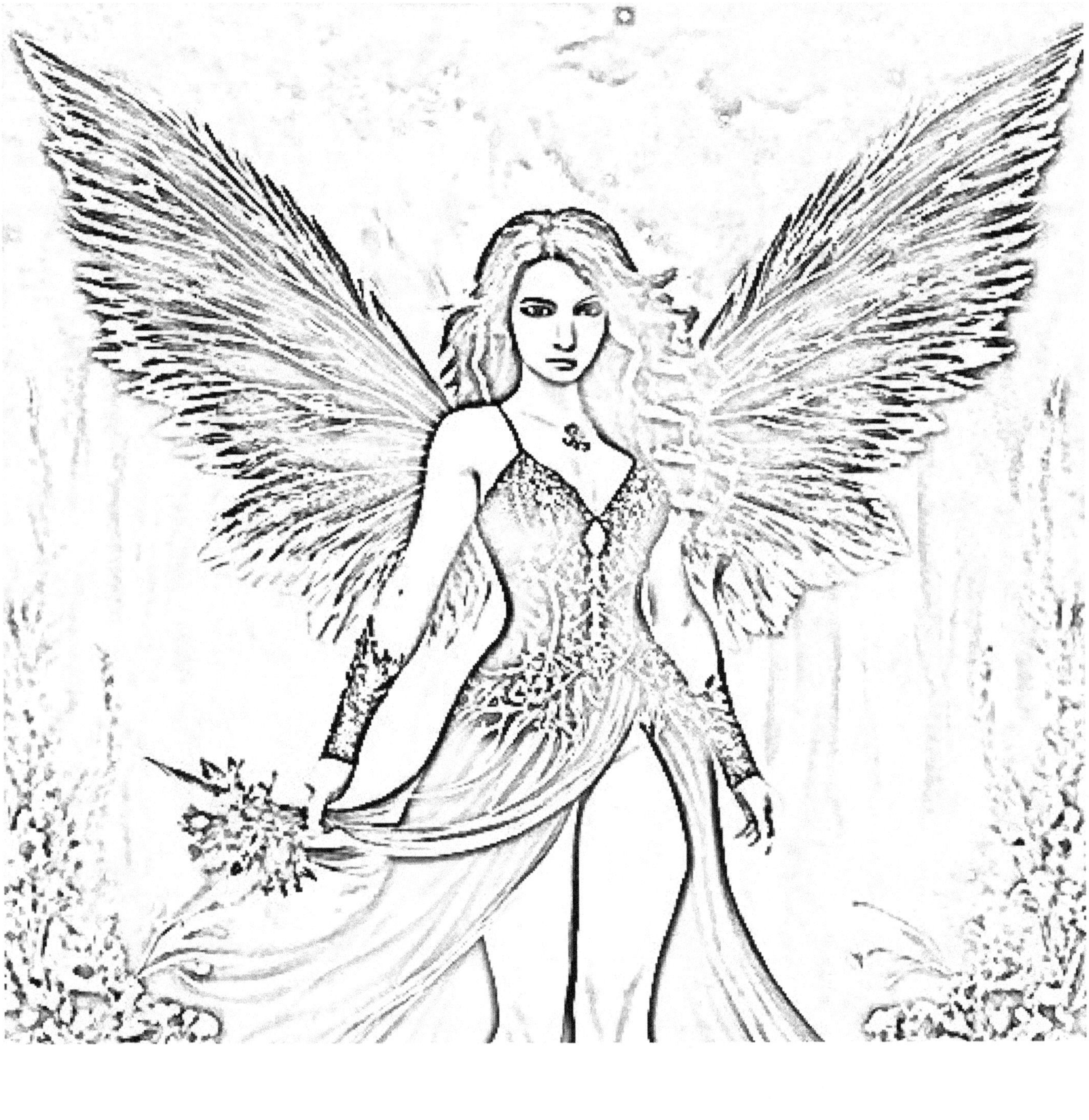

This page is intentionally left blank for bleed through

Pretty Kitties

A book about Dlveristy

K. Rose

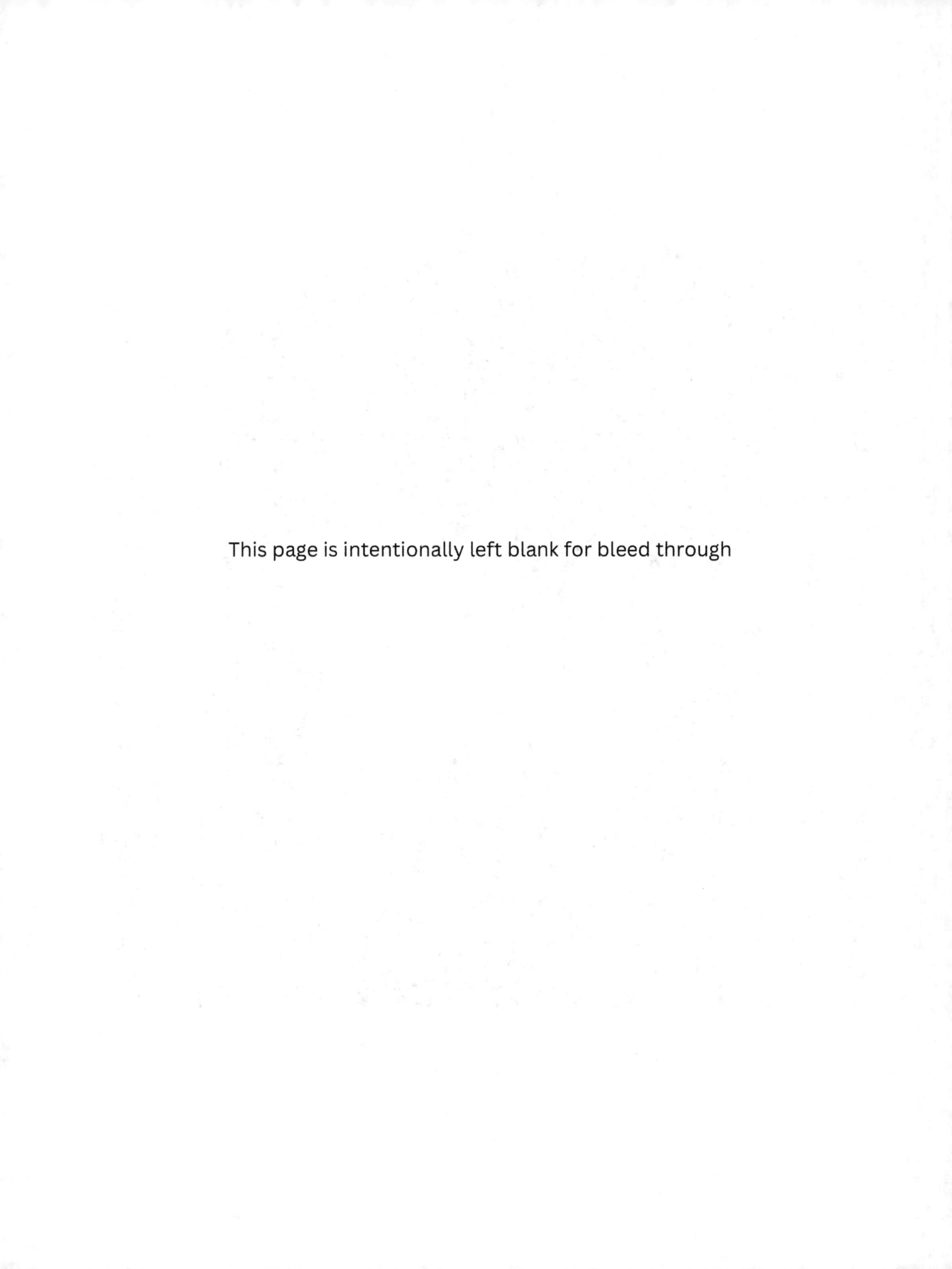

This page is intentionally left blank for bleed through

IN THE HEART OF ICE,
A GLIMMER OF ETERNAL LIFE

BIMINI

INTERNATIONAL BEST SELLING AUTHOR

K. ROSE

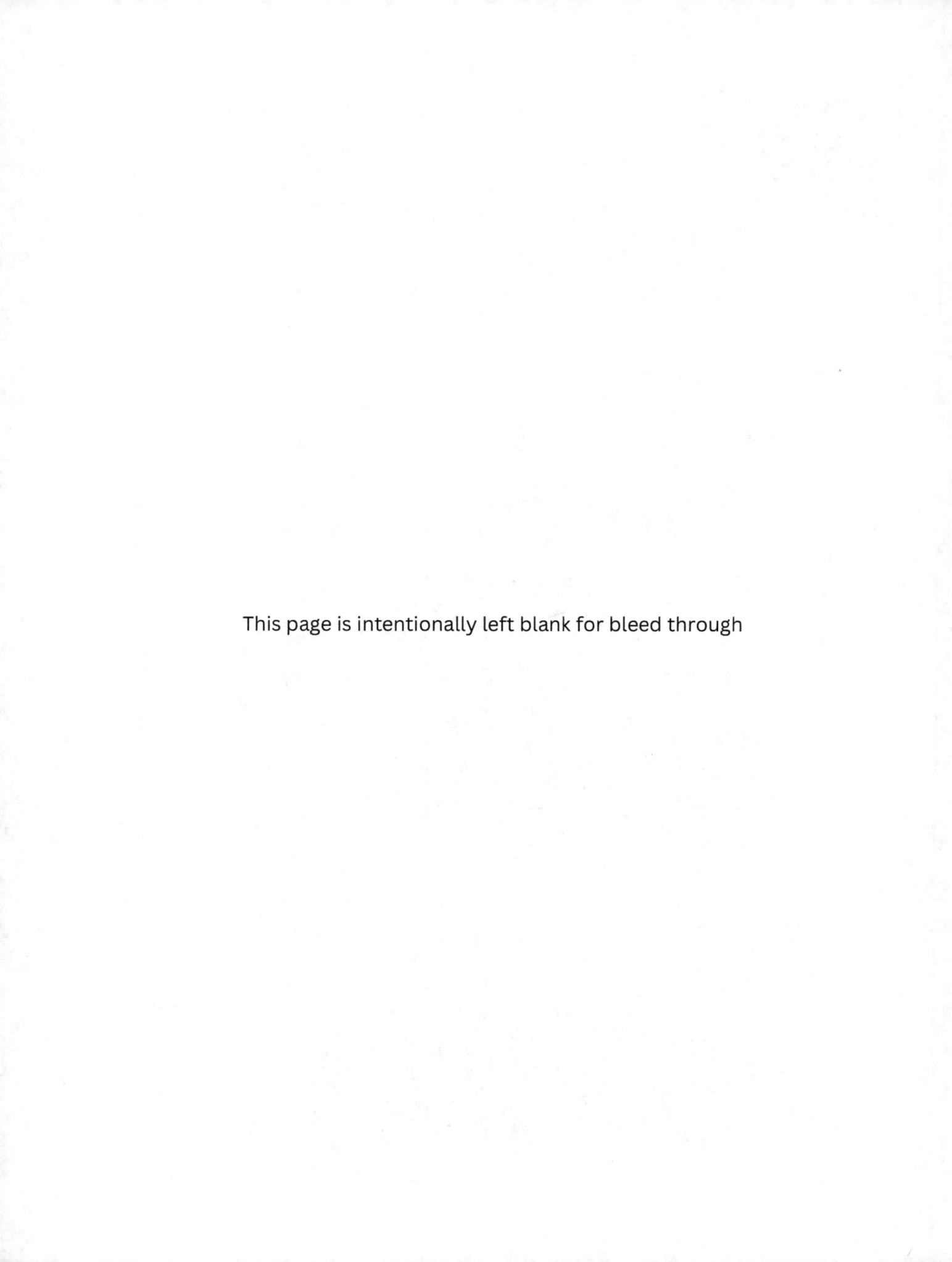

This page is intentionally left blank for bleed through

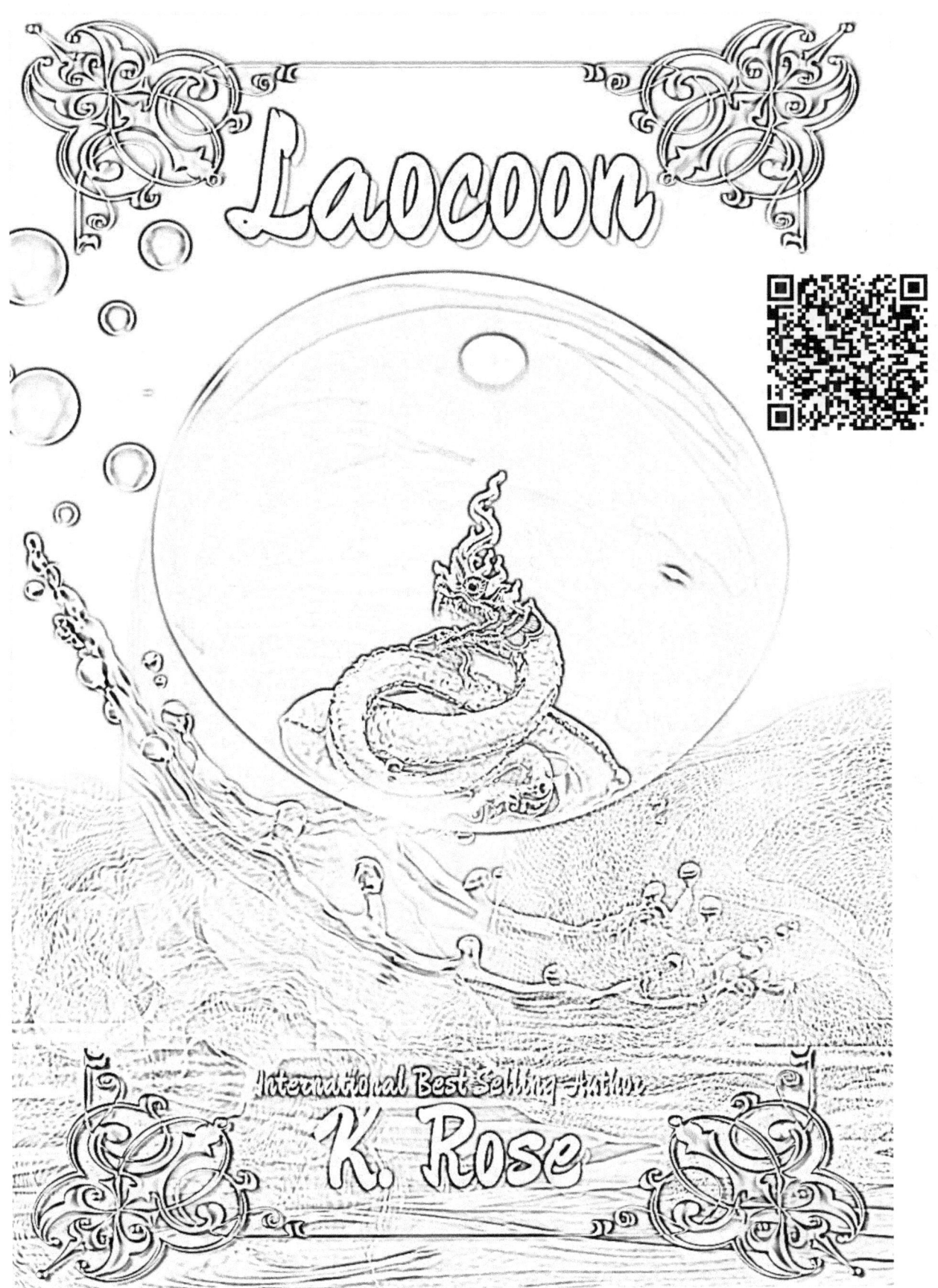

This page is intentionally left blank for bleed through

Enlil

The Prophecy of the Water Sprite

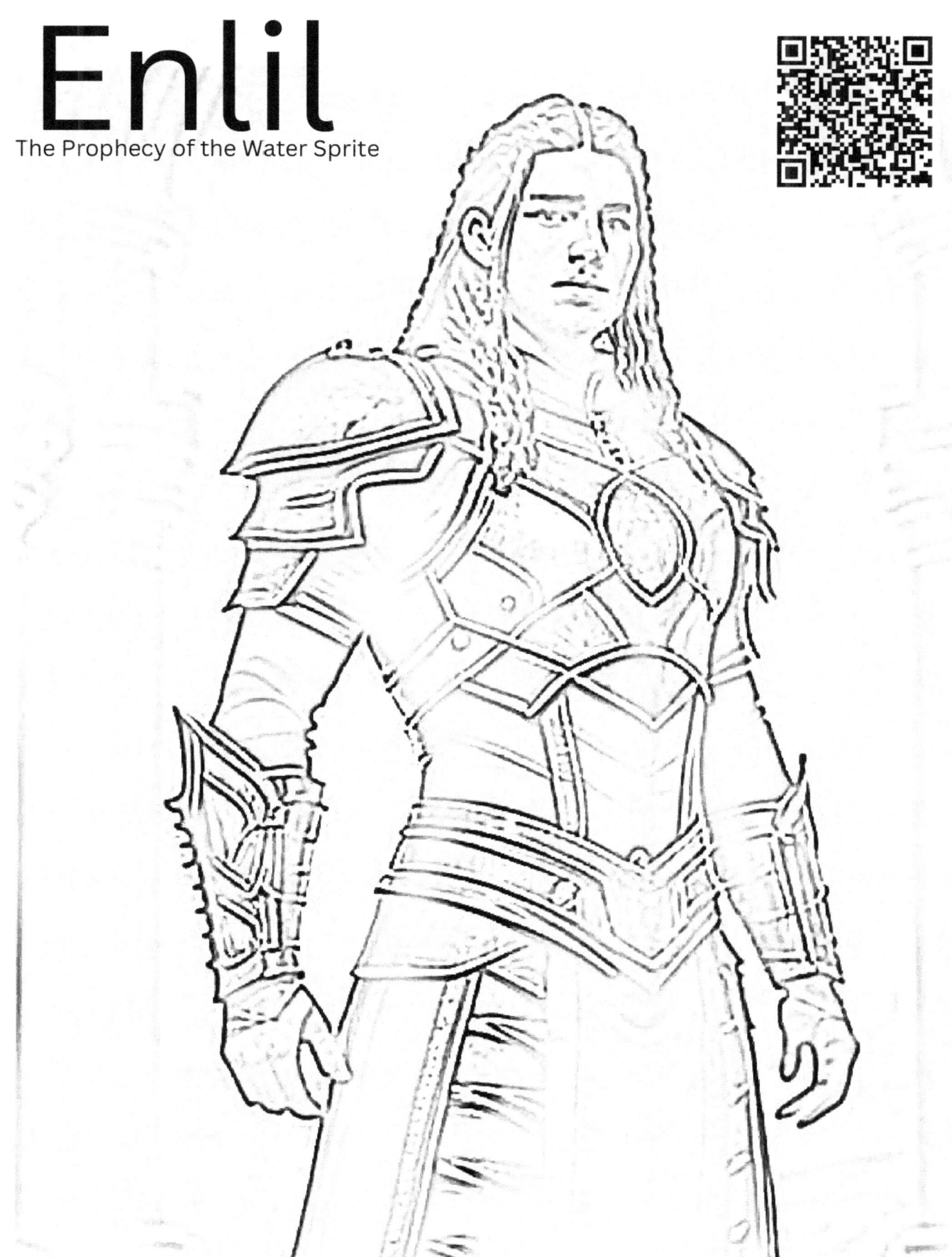

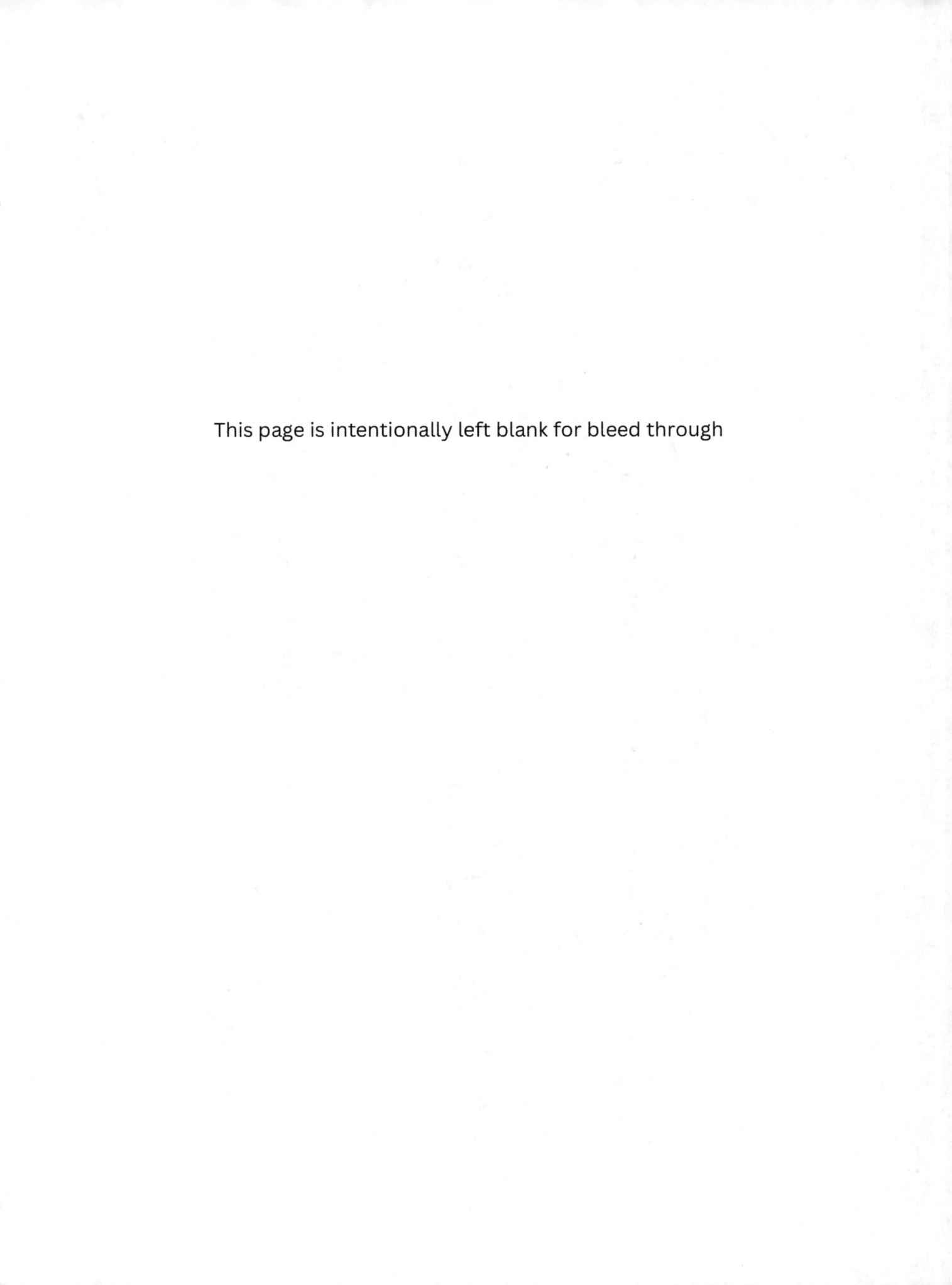

This page is intentionally left blank for bleed through

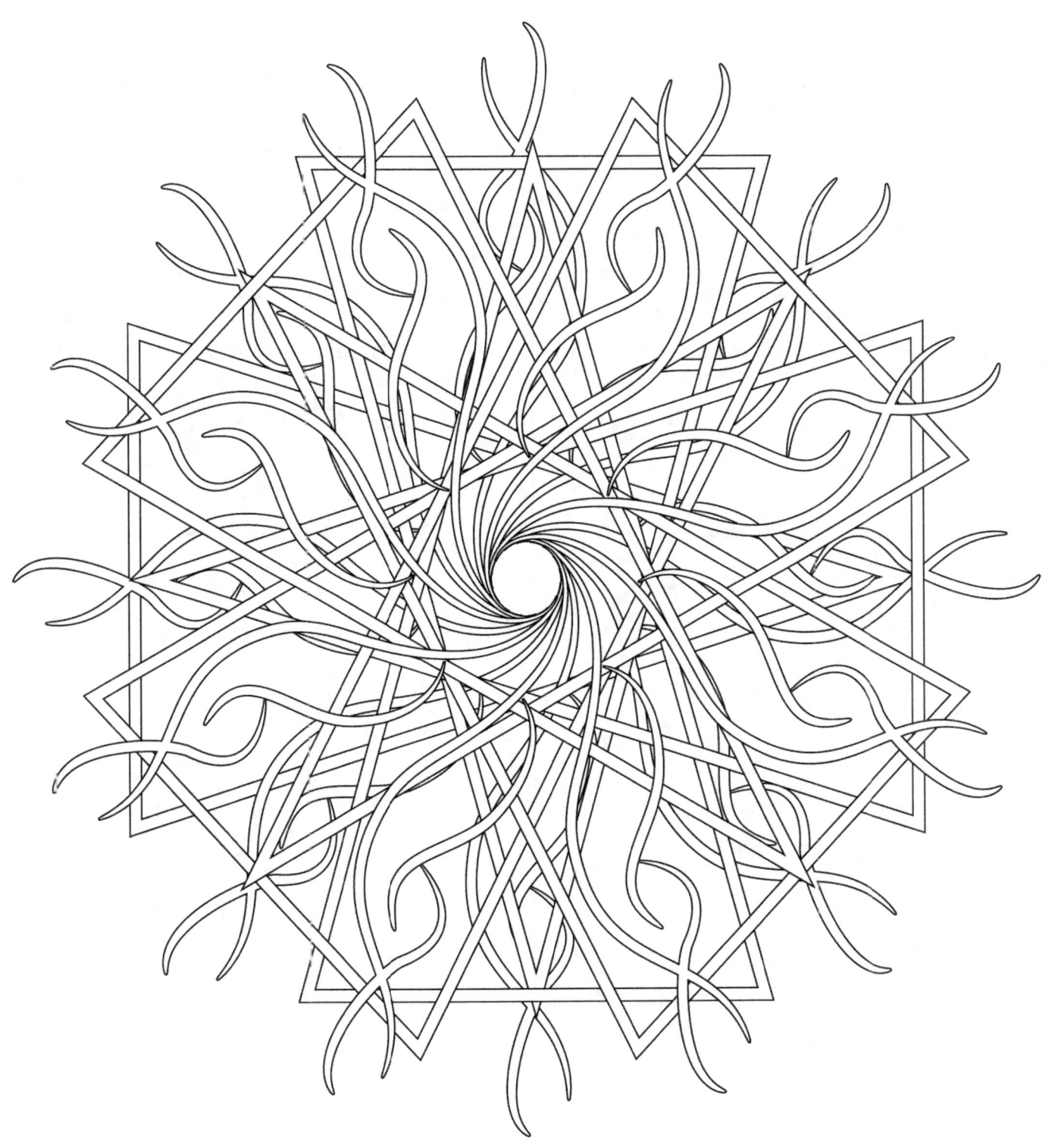

This page is intentionally left blank for bleed through

THE TIGER'S CURSE

INTERNATIONAL BEST SELLING AUTHOR

K. ROSE

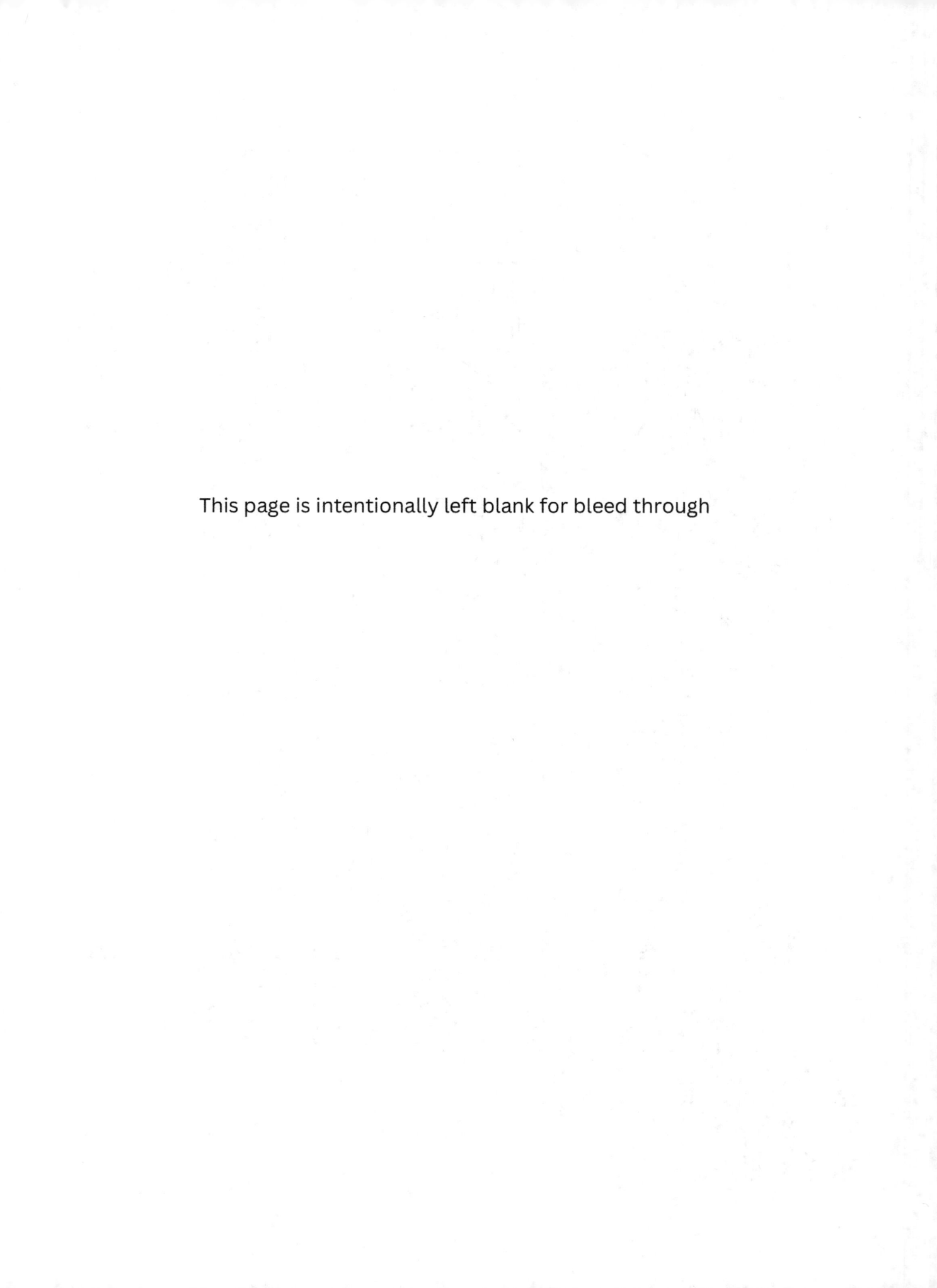

This page is intentionally left blank for bleed through

Skeleton Under The Lamp

International Best Selling Author

K. Rose

This page is intentionally left blank for bleed through

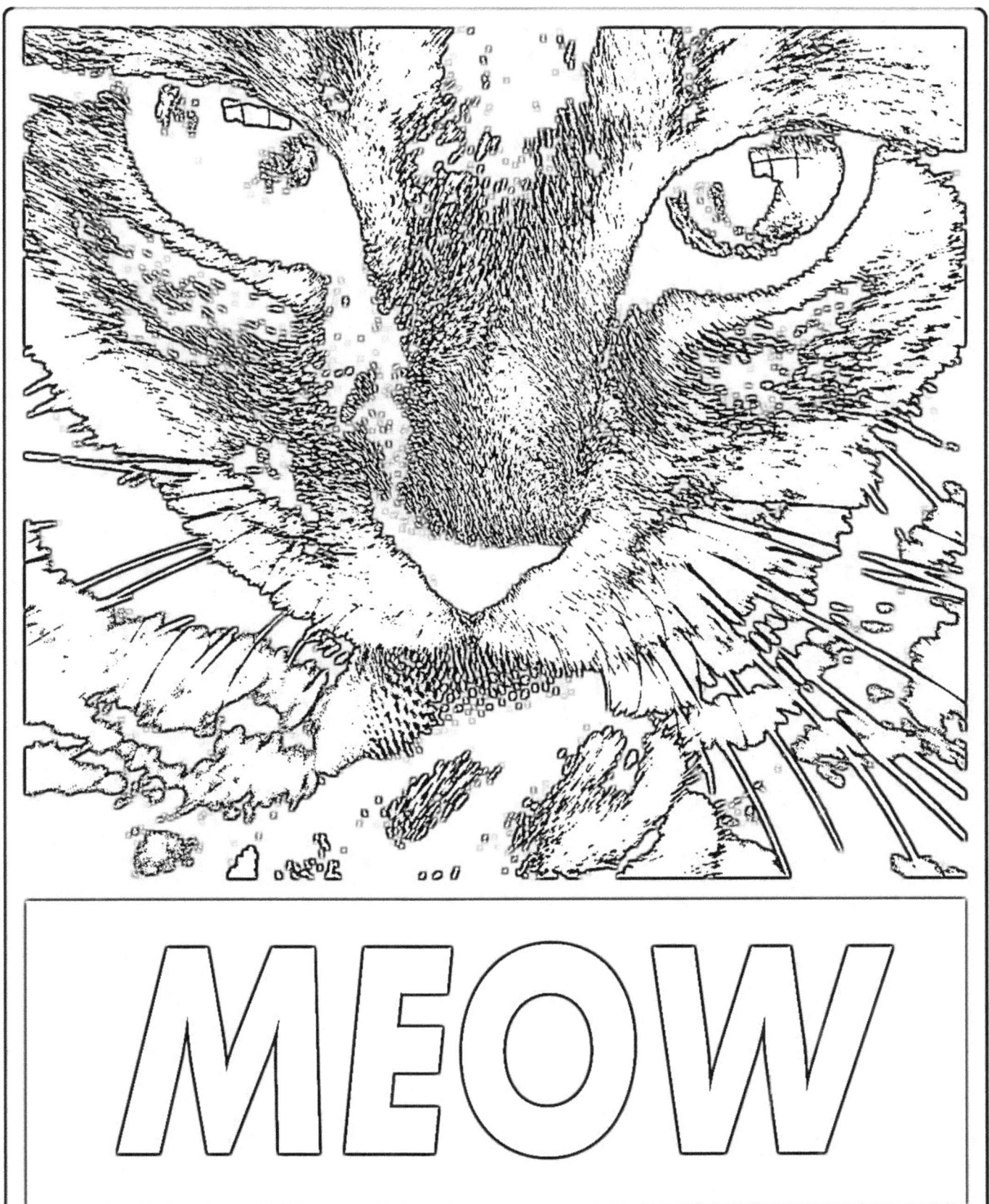

This page is intentionally left blank for bleed through

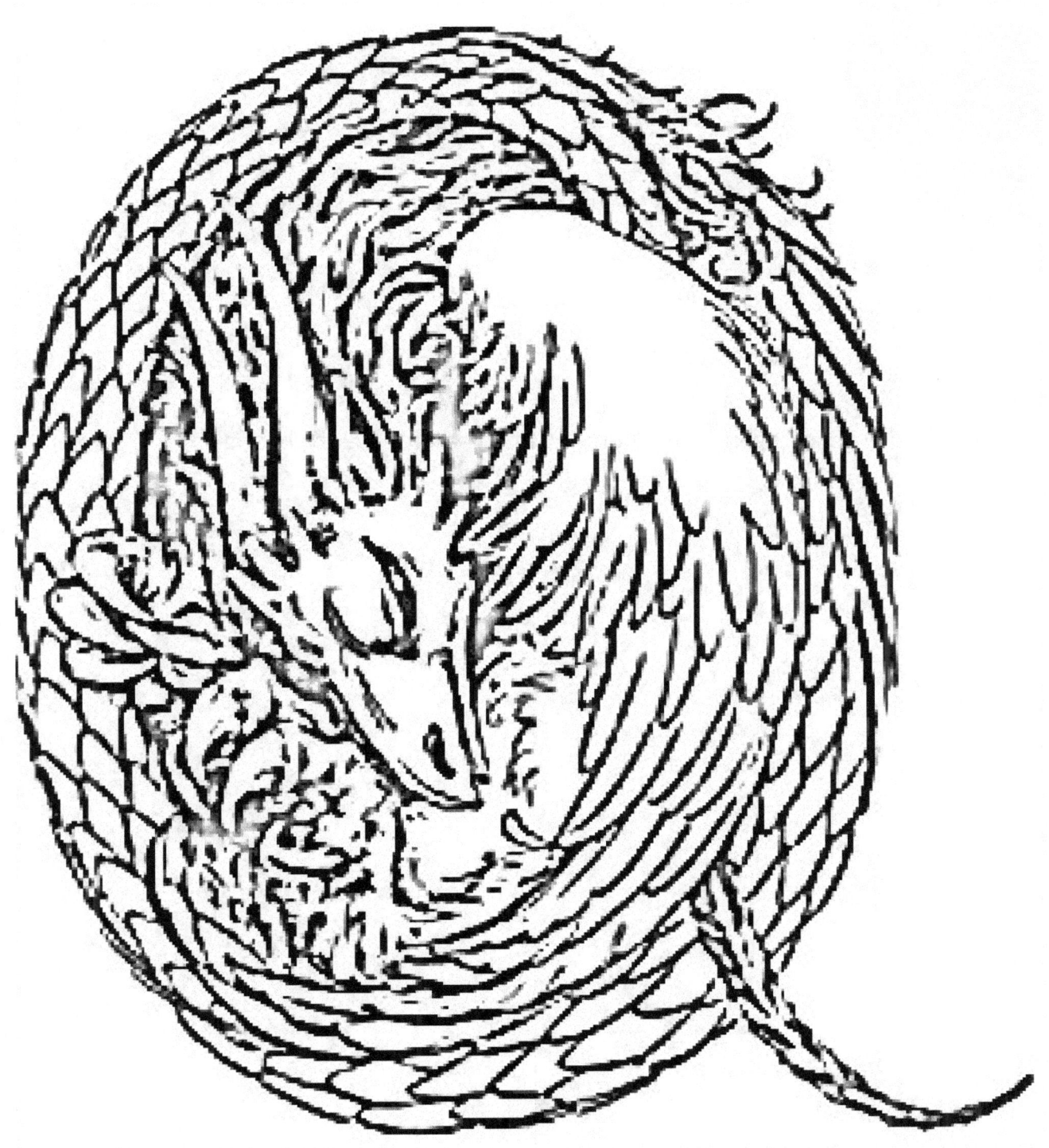

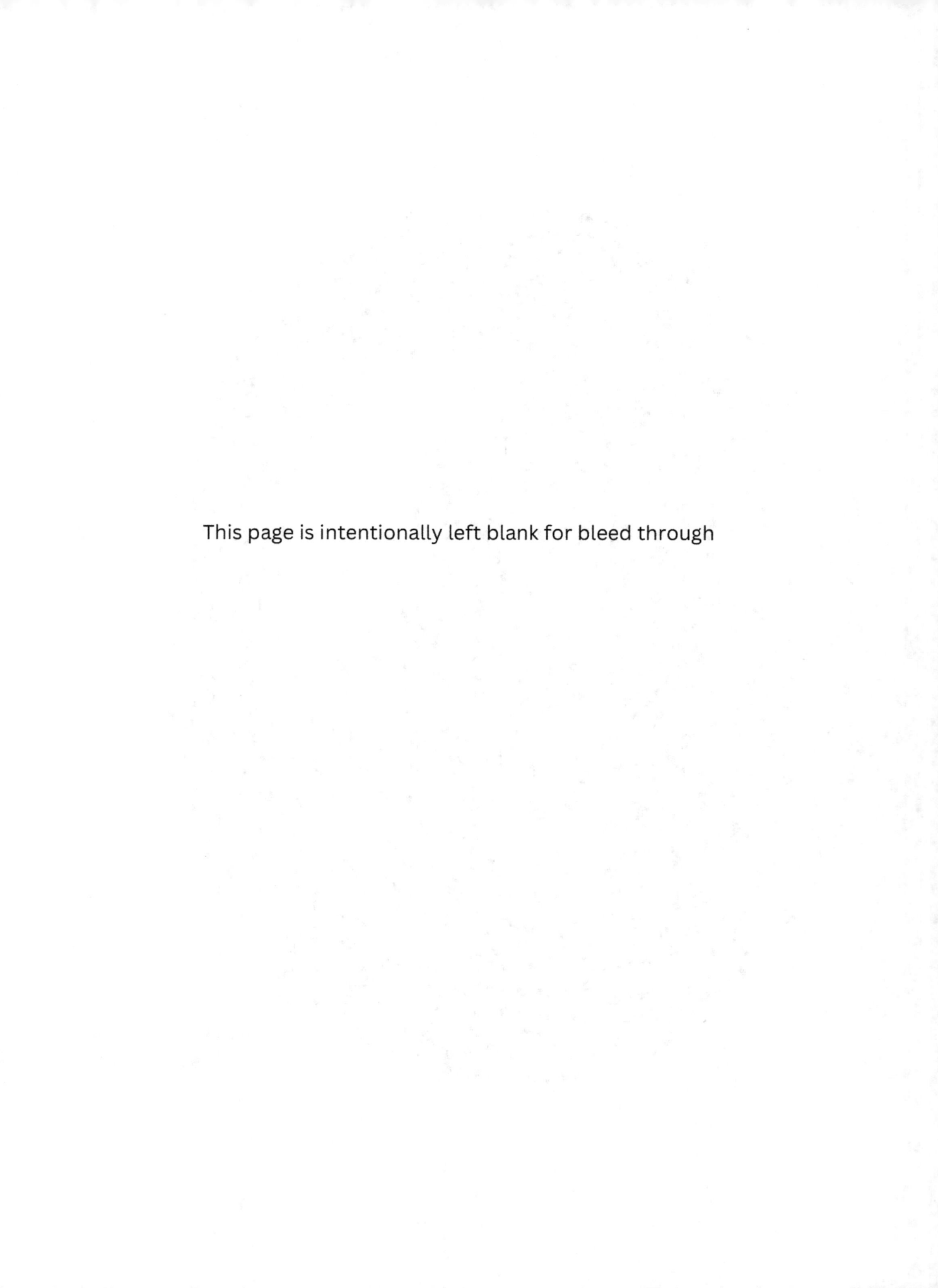

This page is intentionally left blank for bleed through

I REALLY TRIED
TO BEHAVE

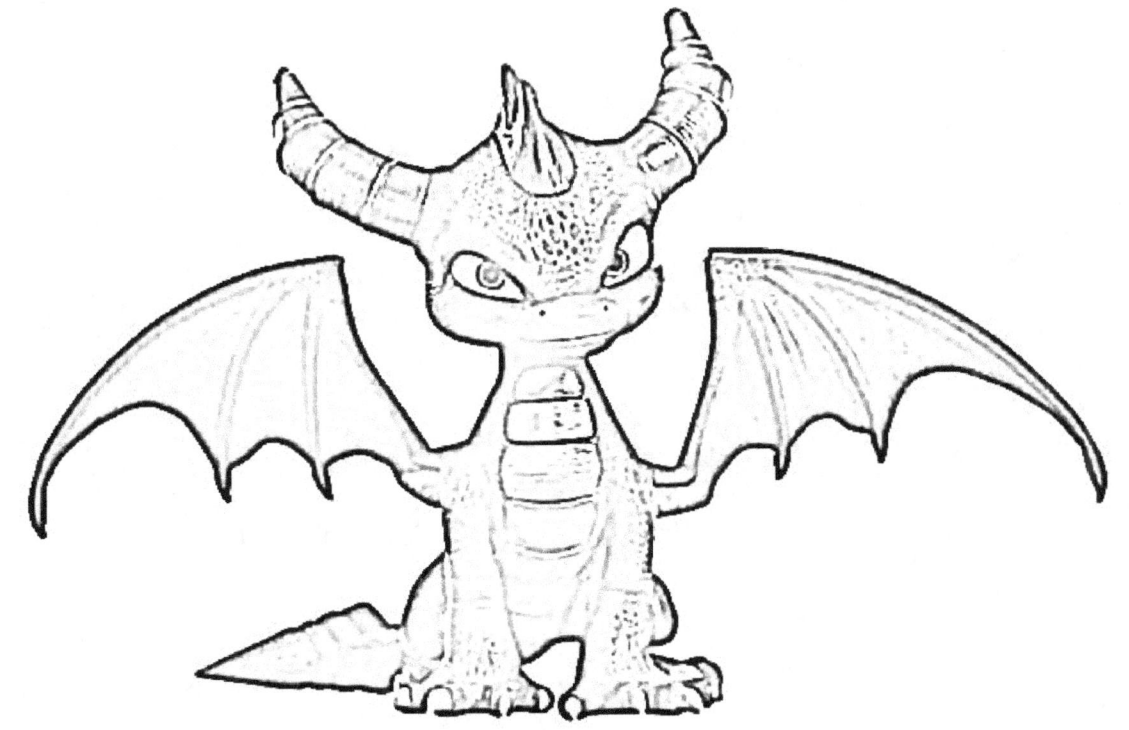

BUT THERE WERE
TOO MANY OTHER OPTIONS

This page is intentionally left blank for bleed through

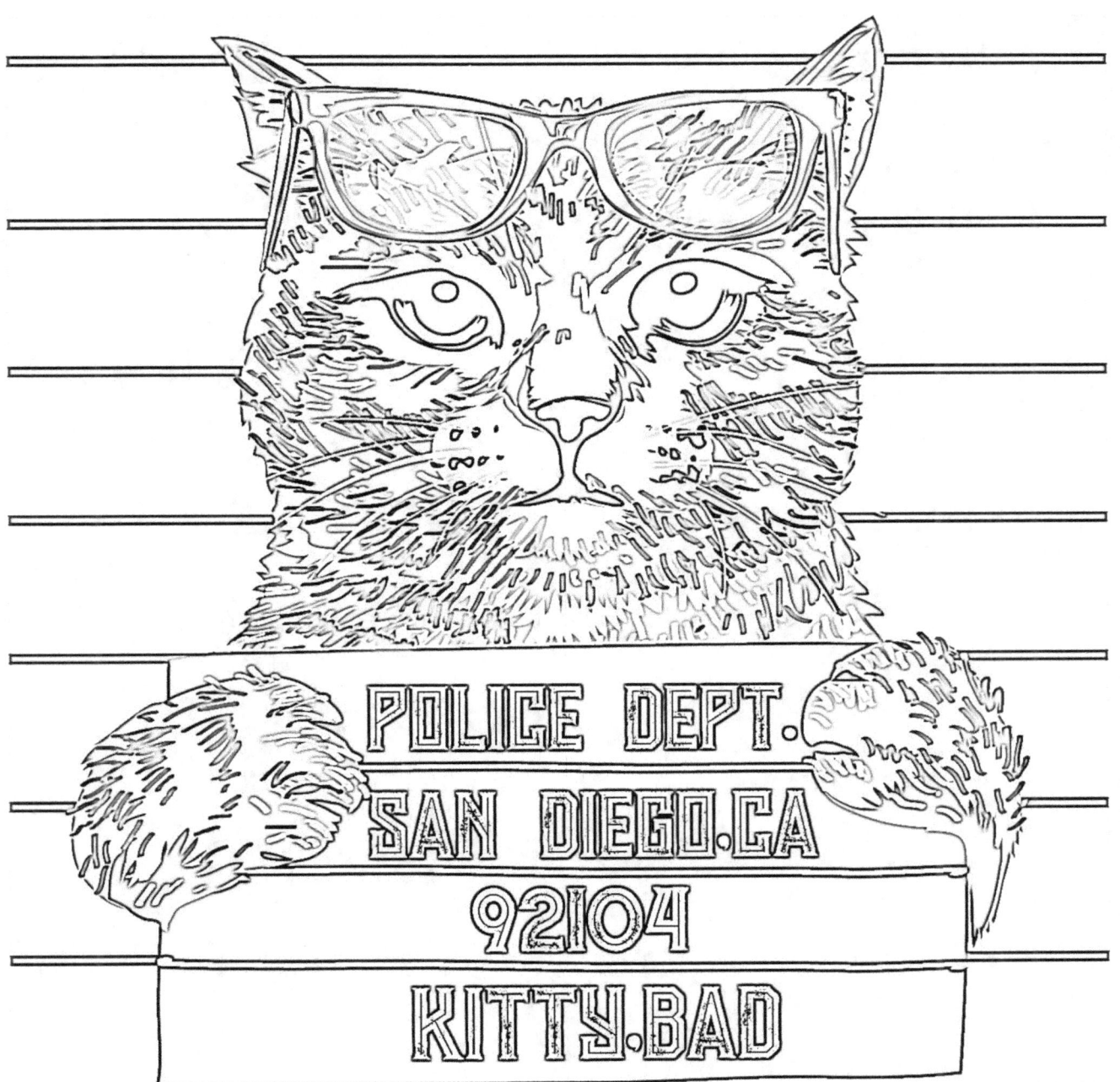

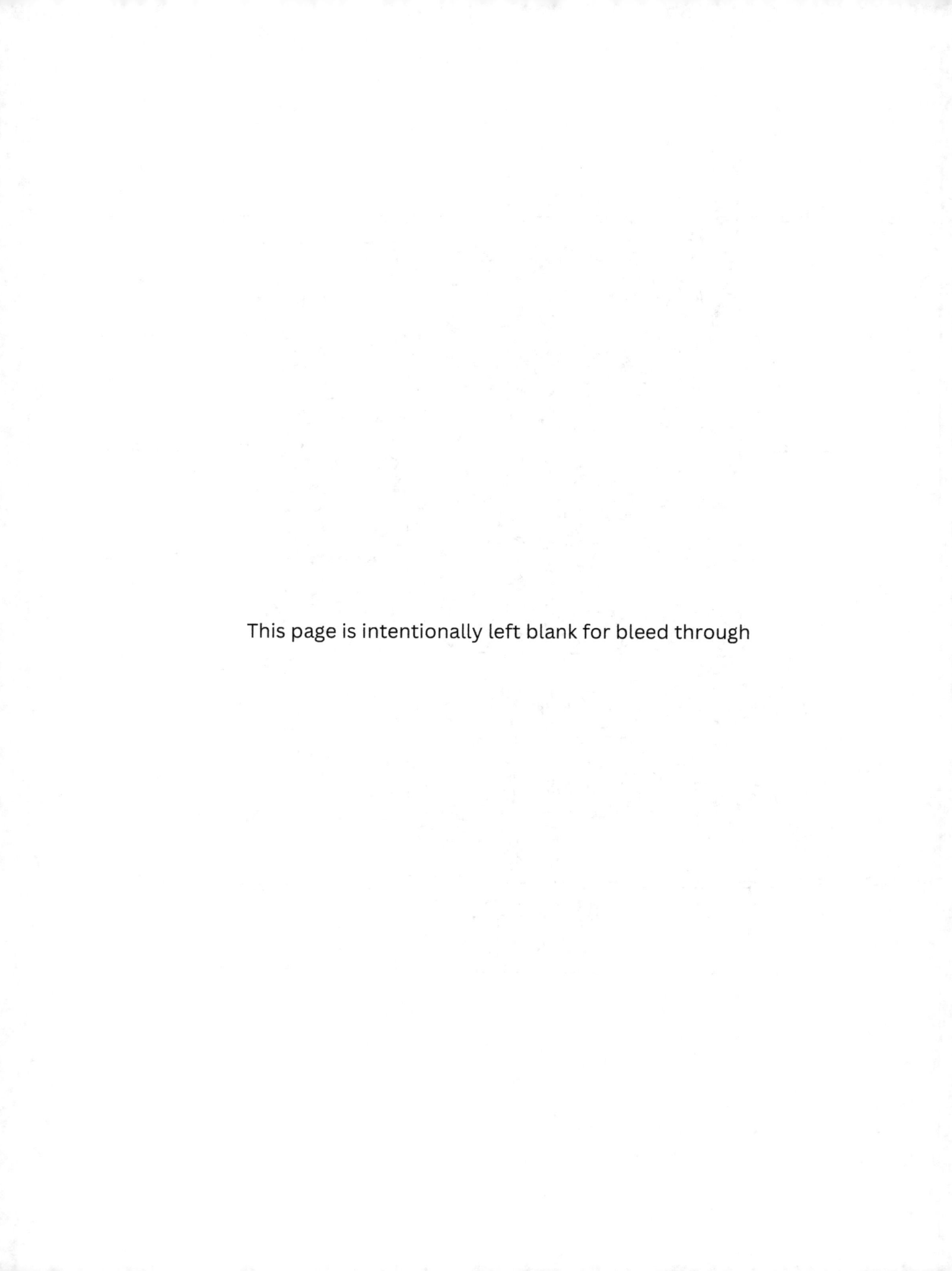

This page is intentionally left blank for bleed through

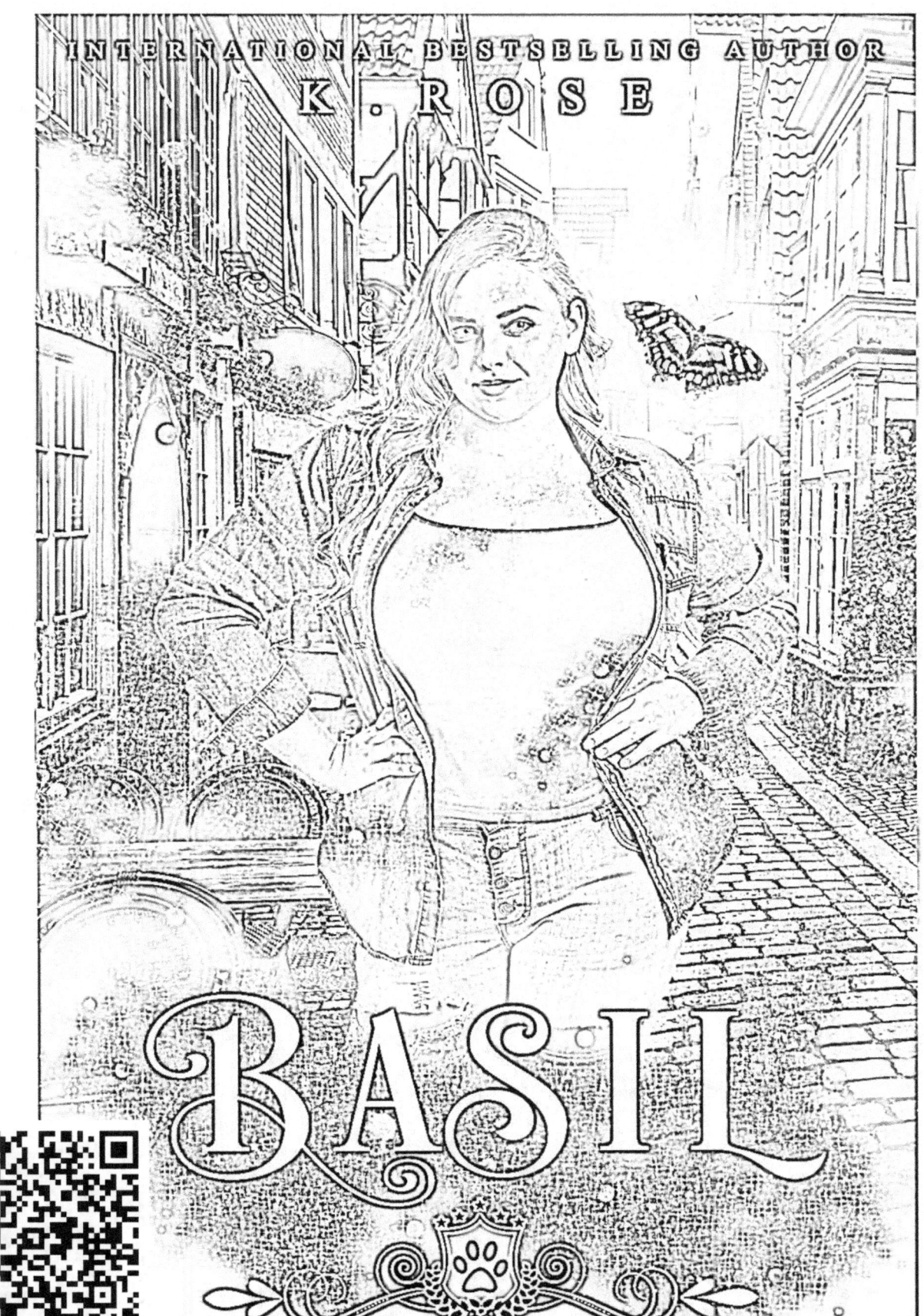

INTERNATIONAL BESTSELLING AUTHOR
K. ROSE

BASIL

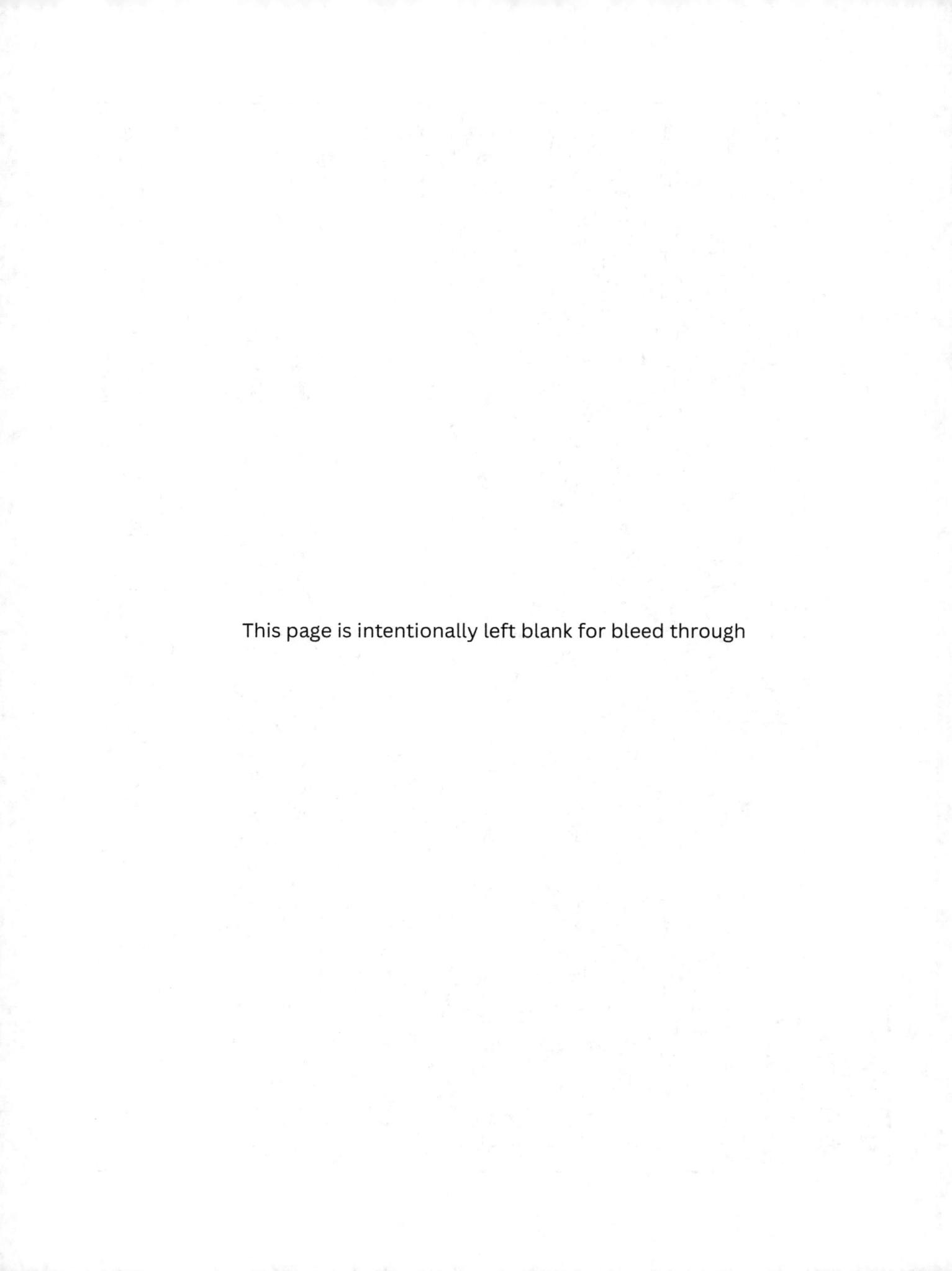

This page is intentionally left blank for bleed through

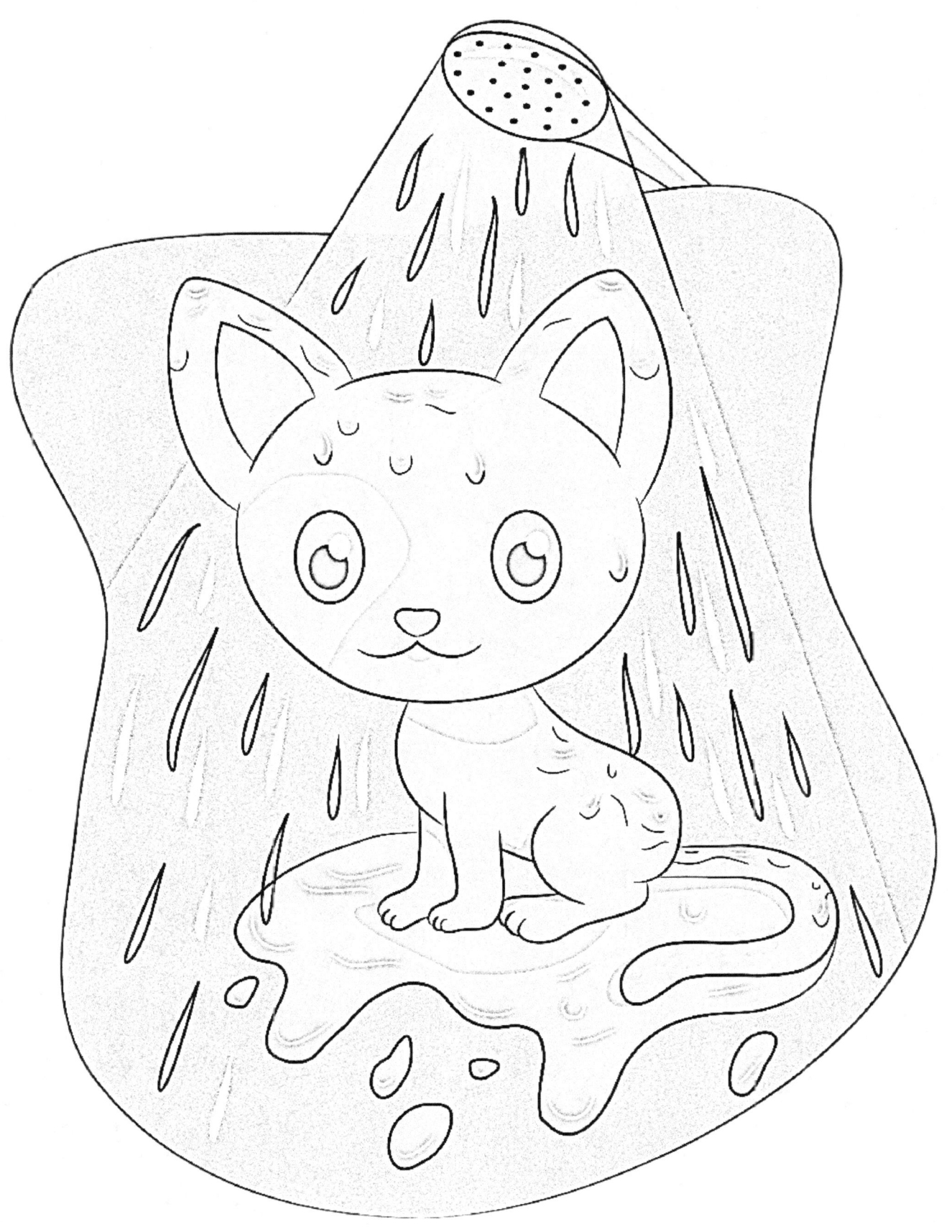

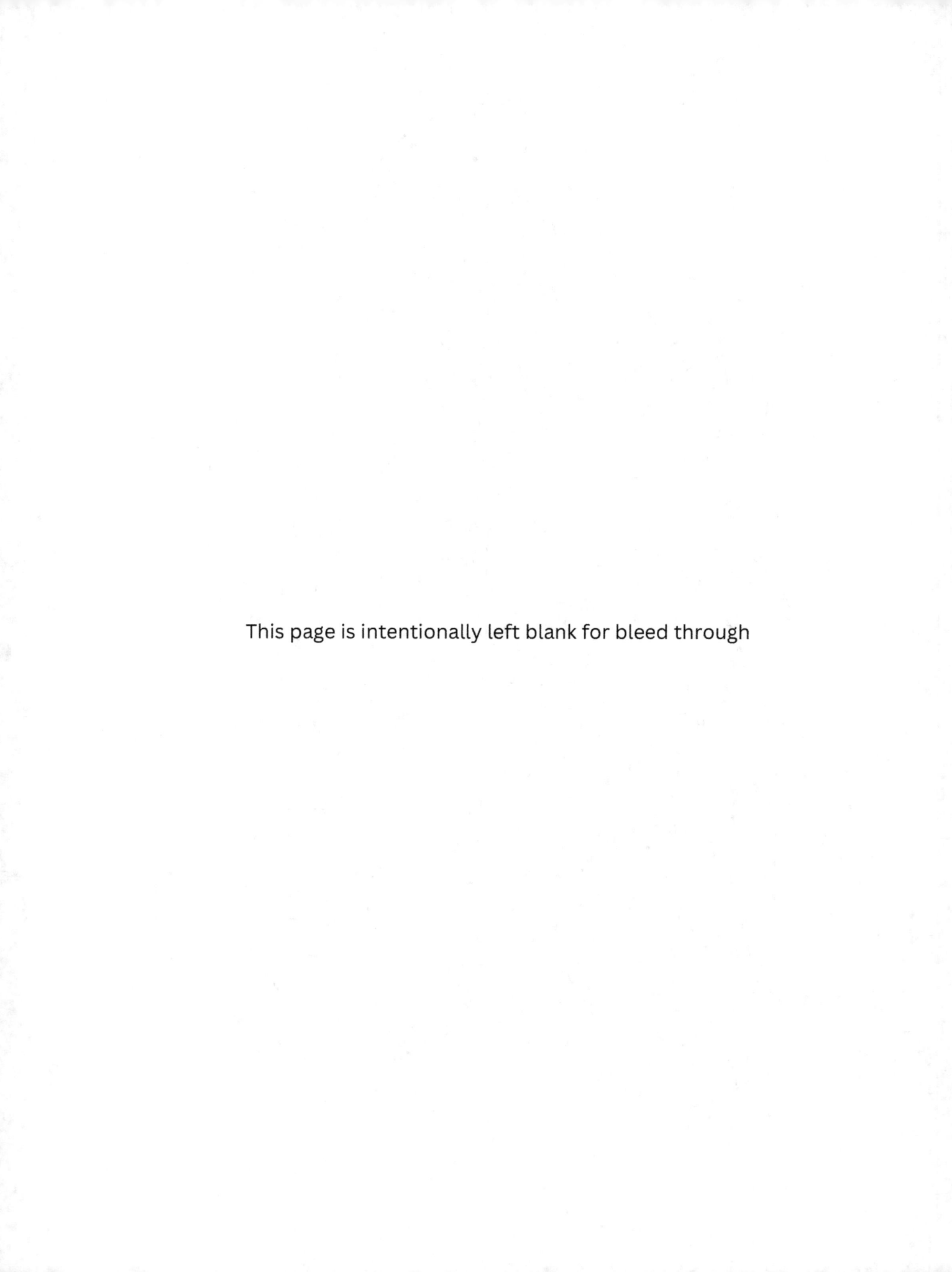

This page is intentionally left blank for bleed through

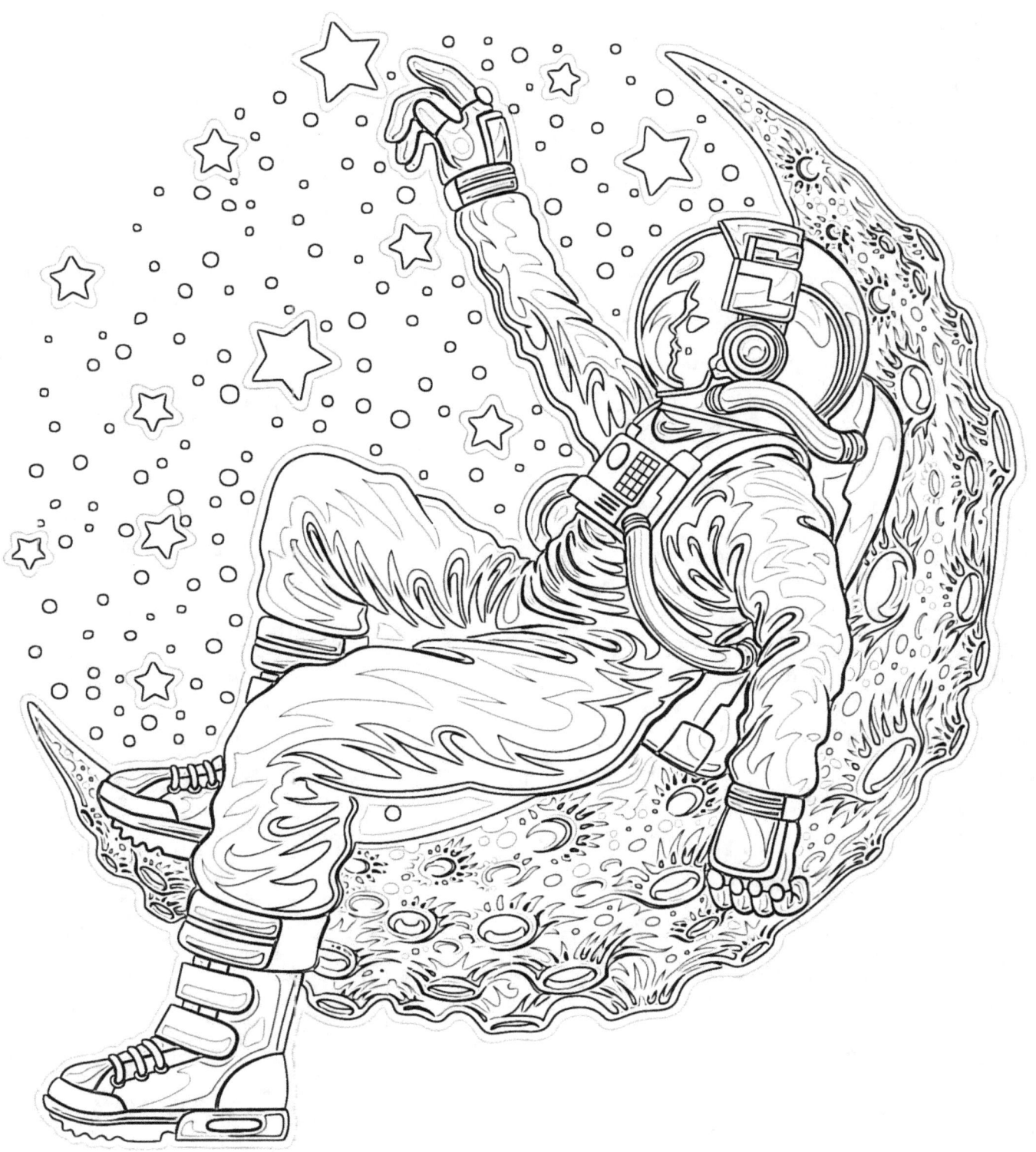

This page is intentionally left blank for bleed through

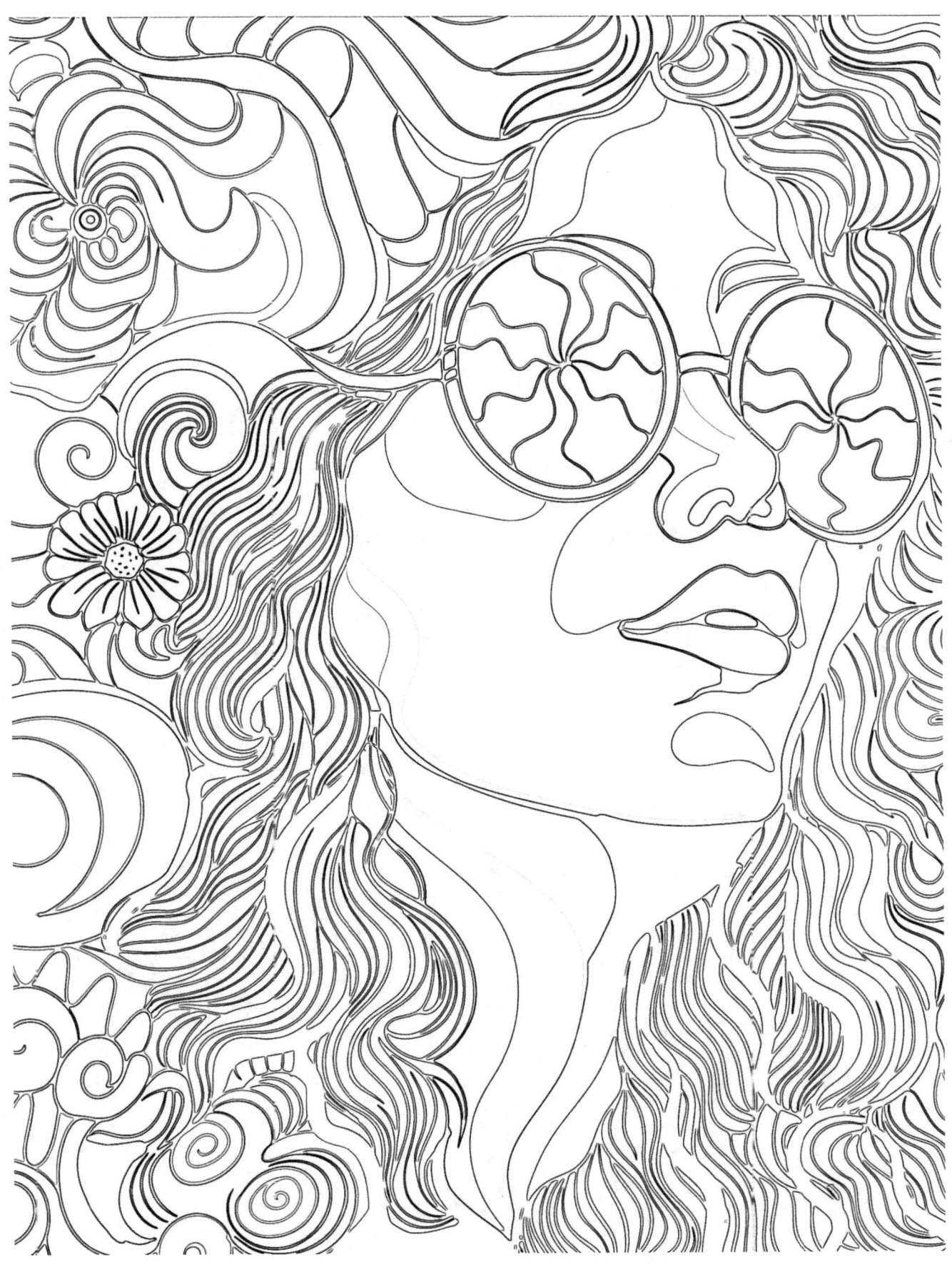

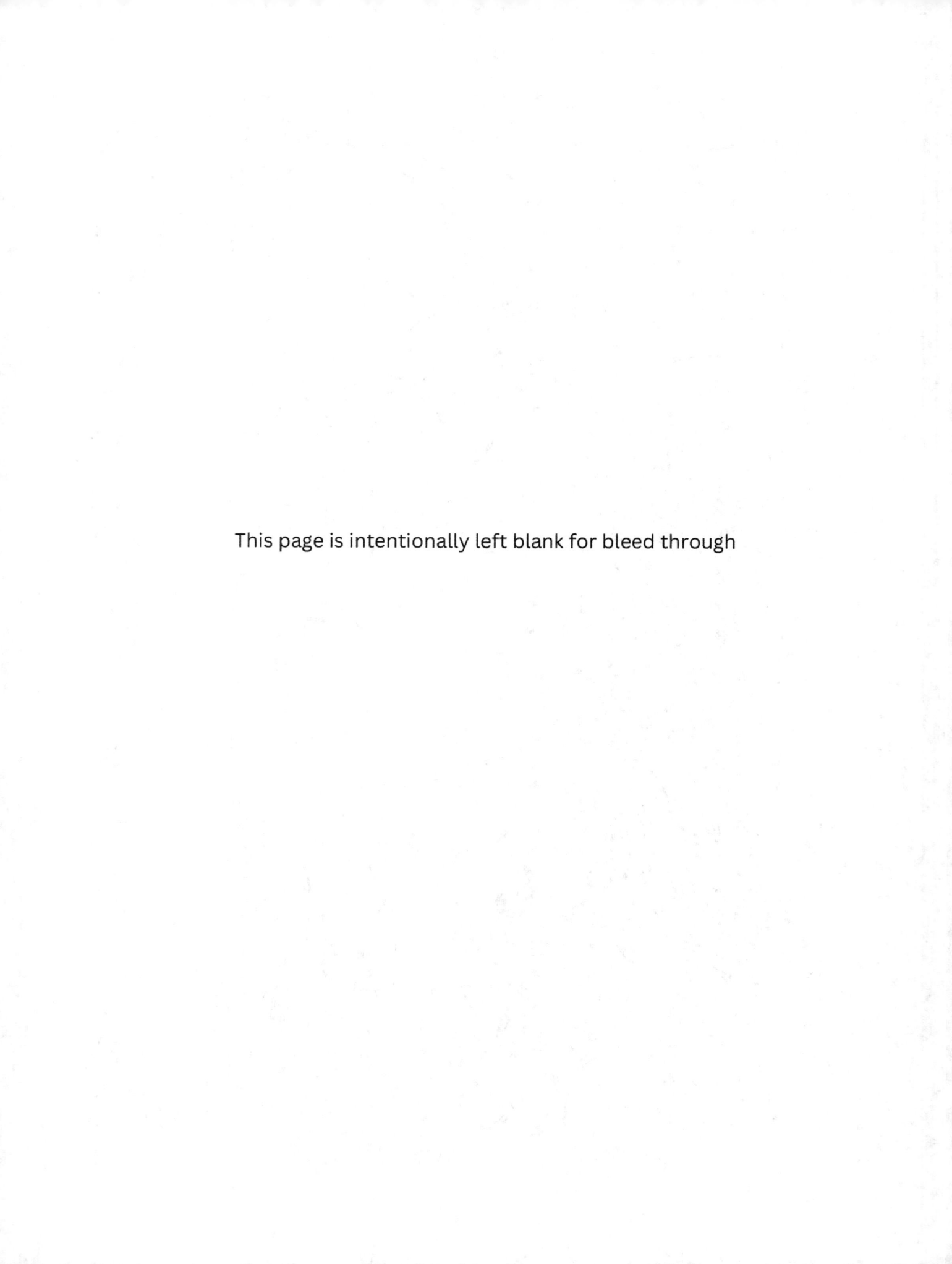

This page is intentionally left blank for bleed through

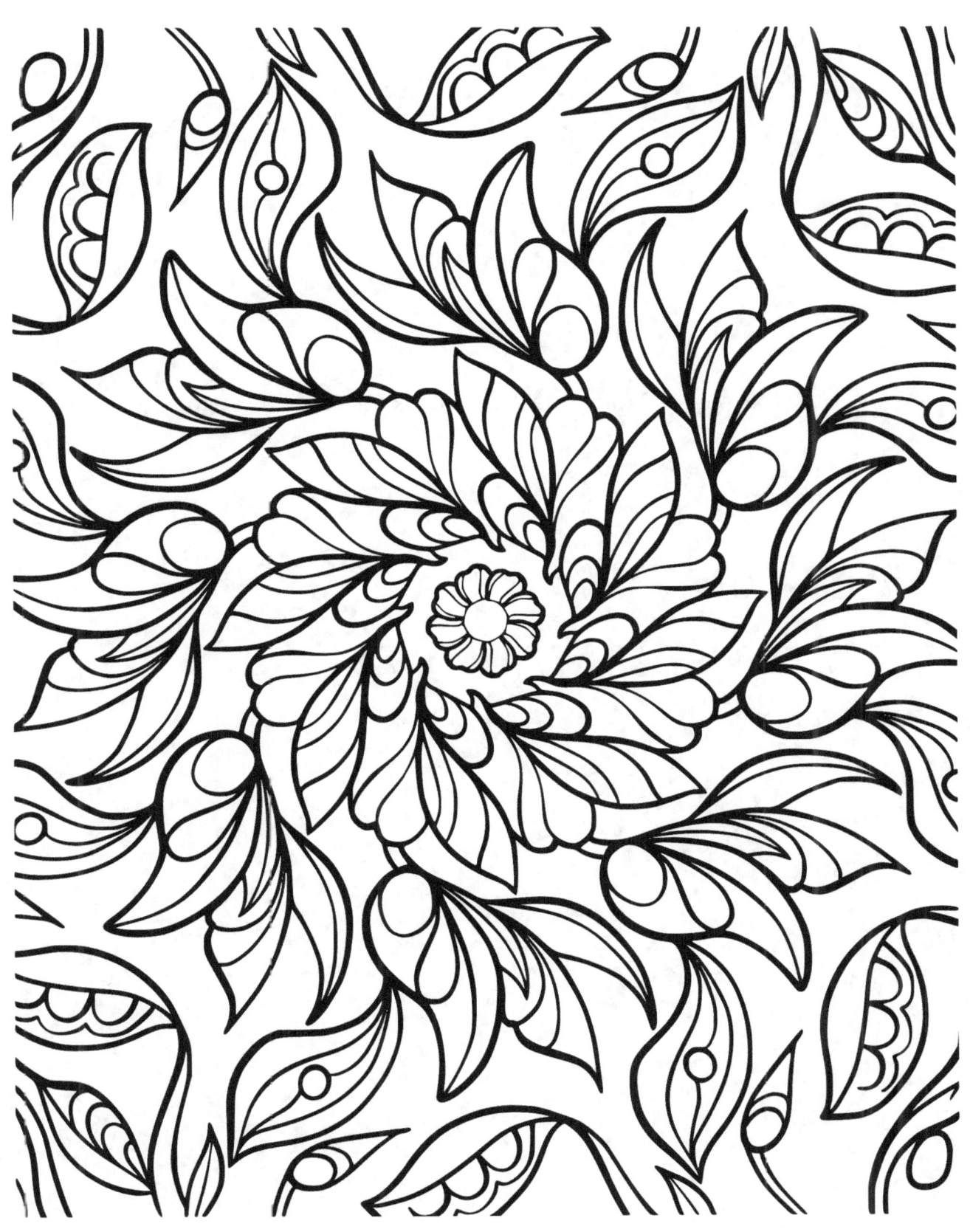

This page is intentionally left blank for bleed through

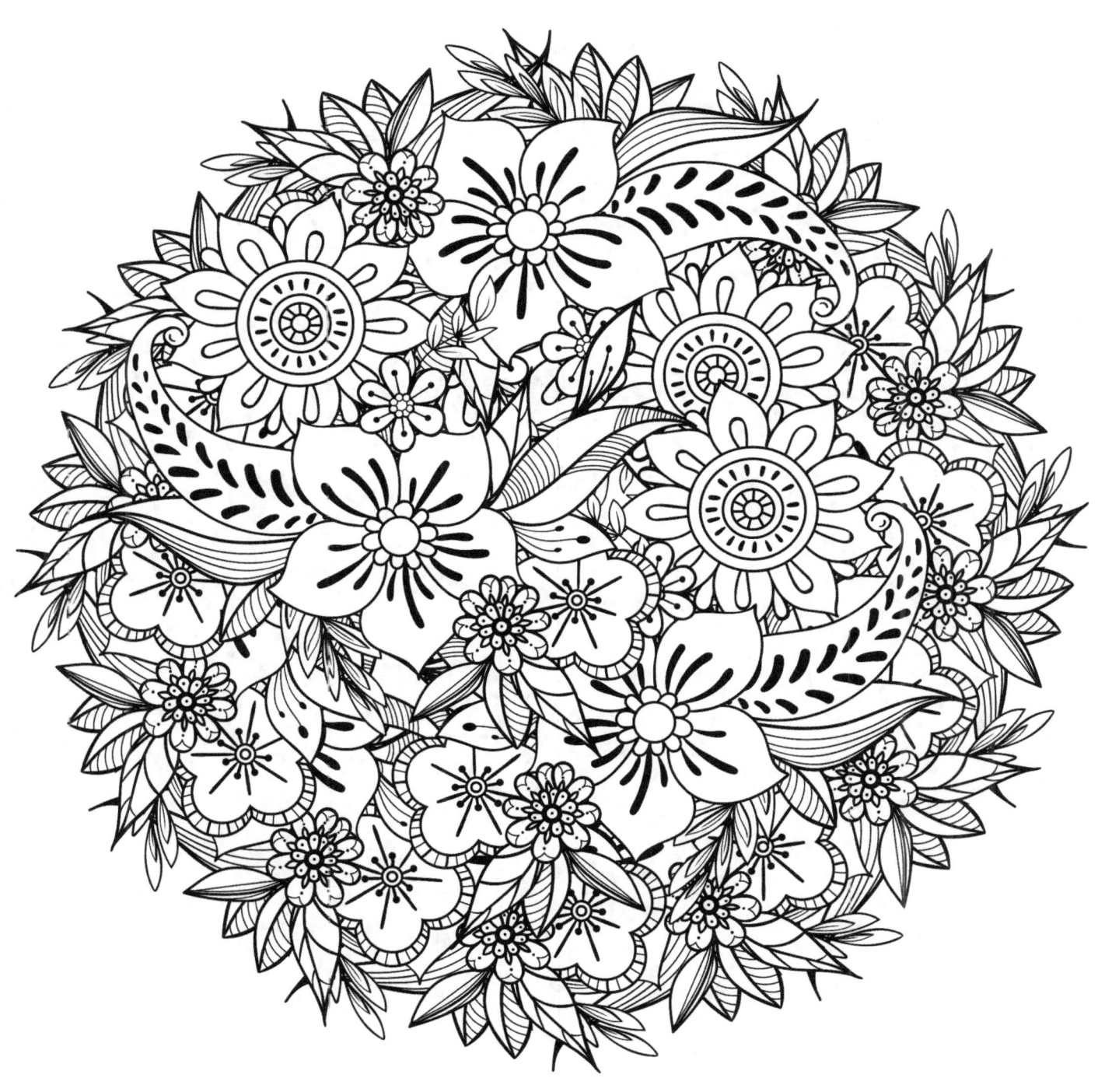

This page is intentionally left blank for bleed through

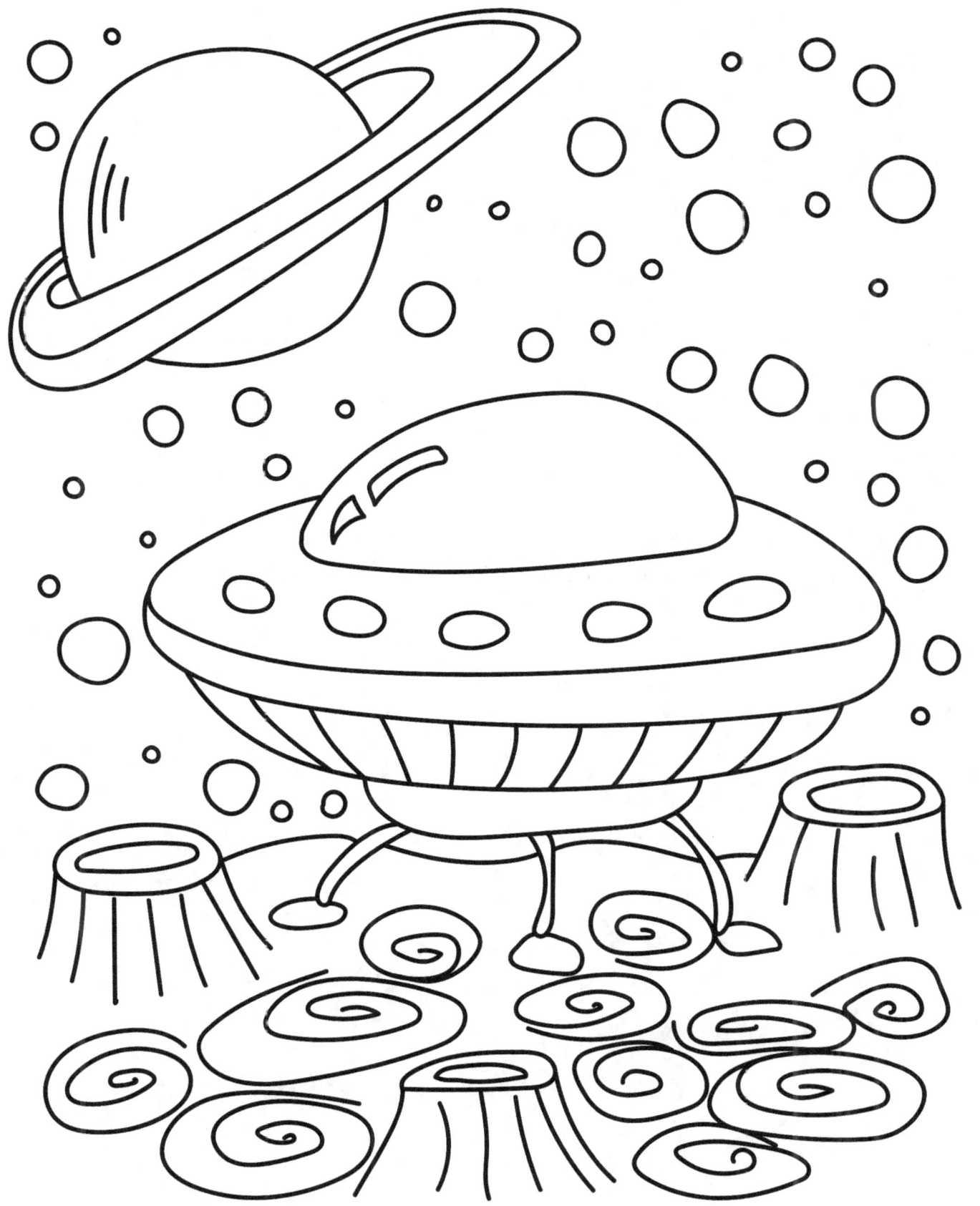

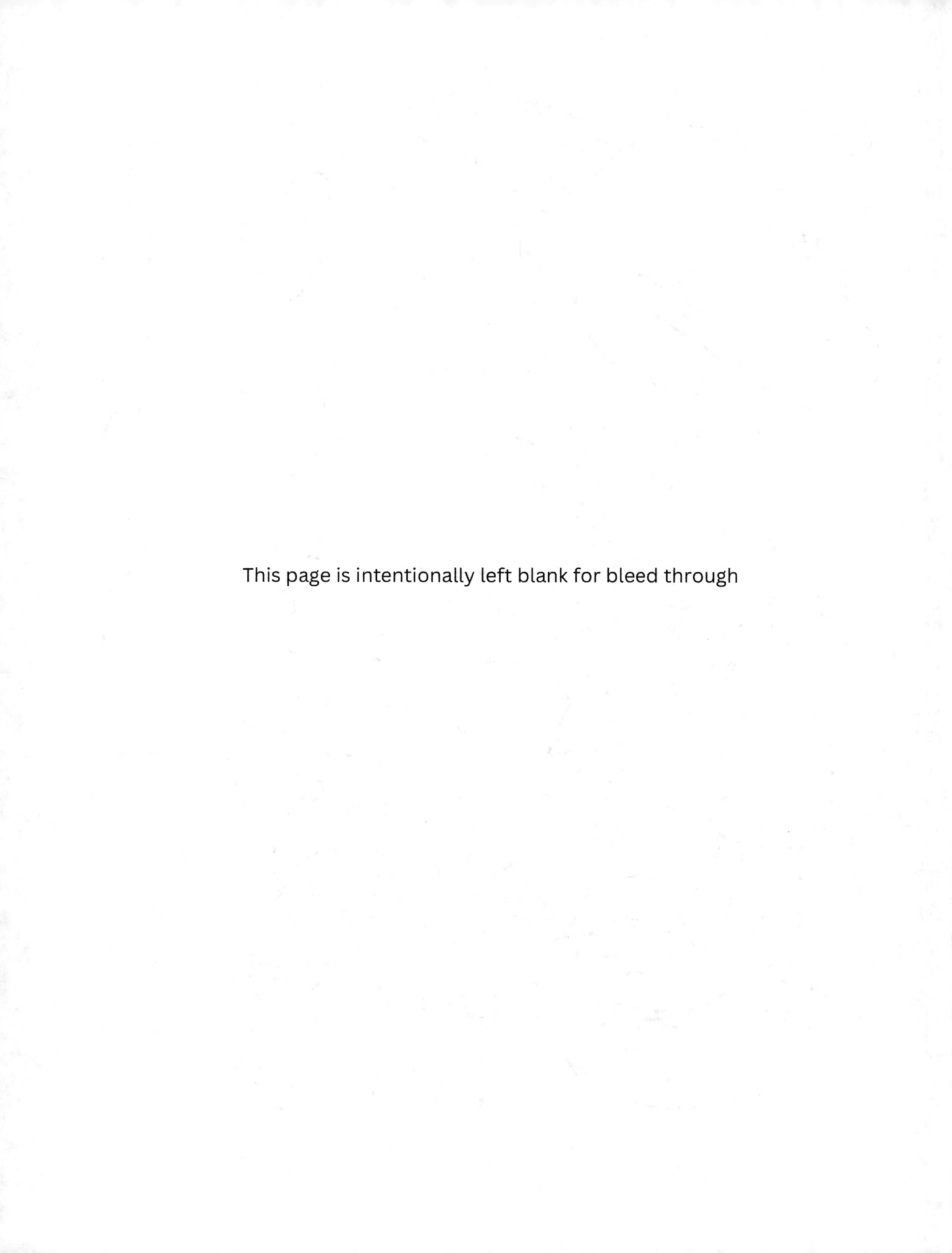

This page is intentionally left blank for bleed through

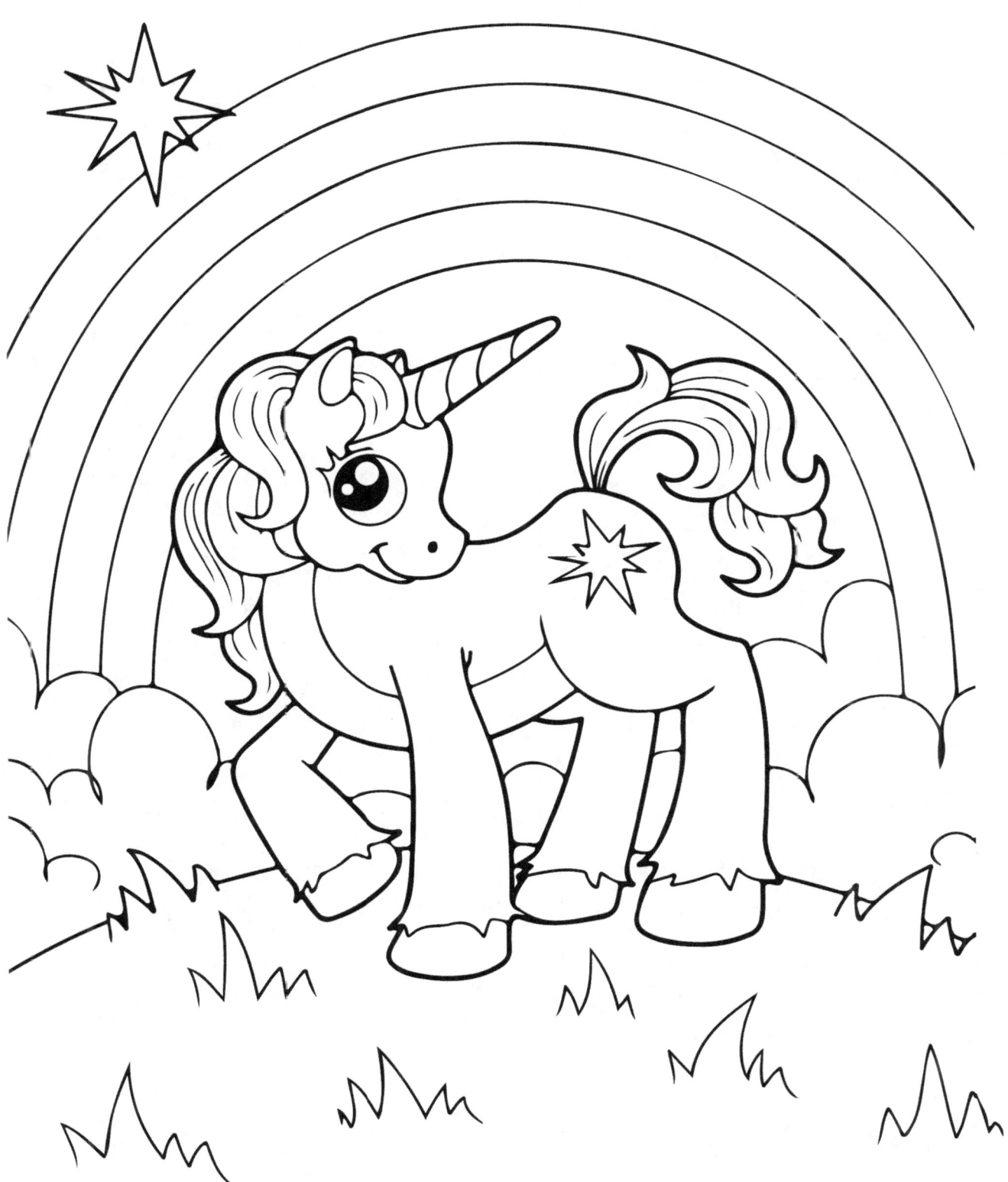

This page is intentionally left blank for bleed through

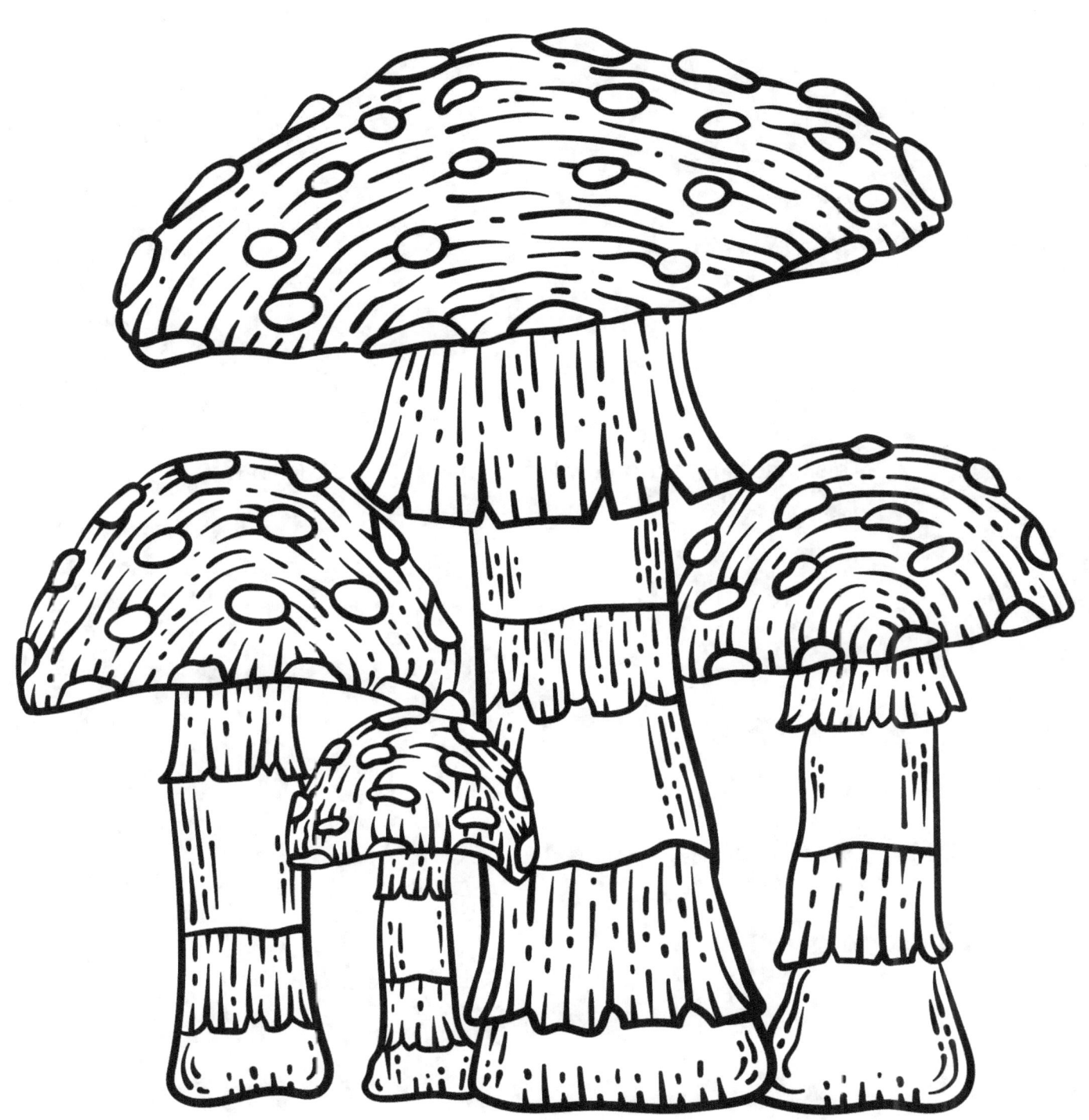

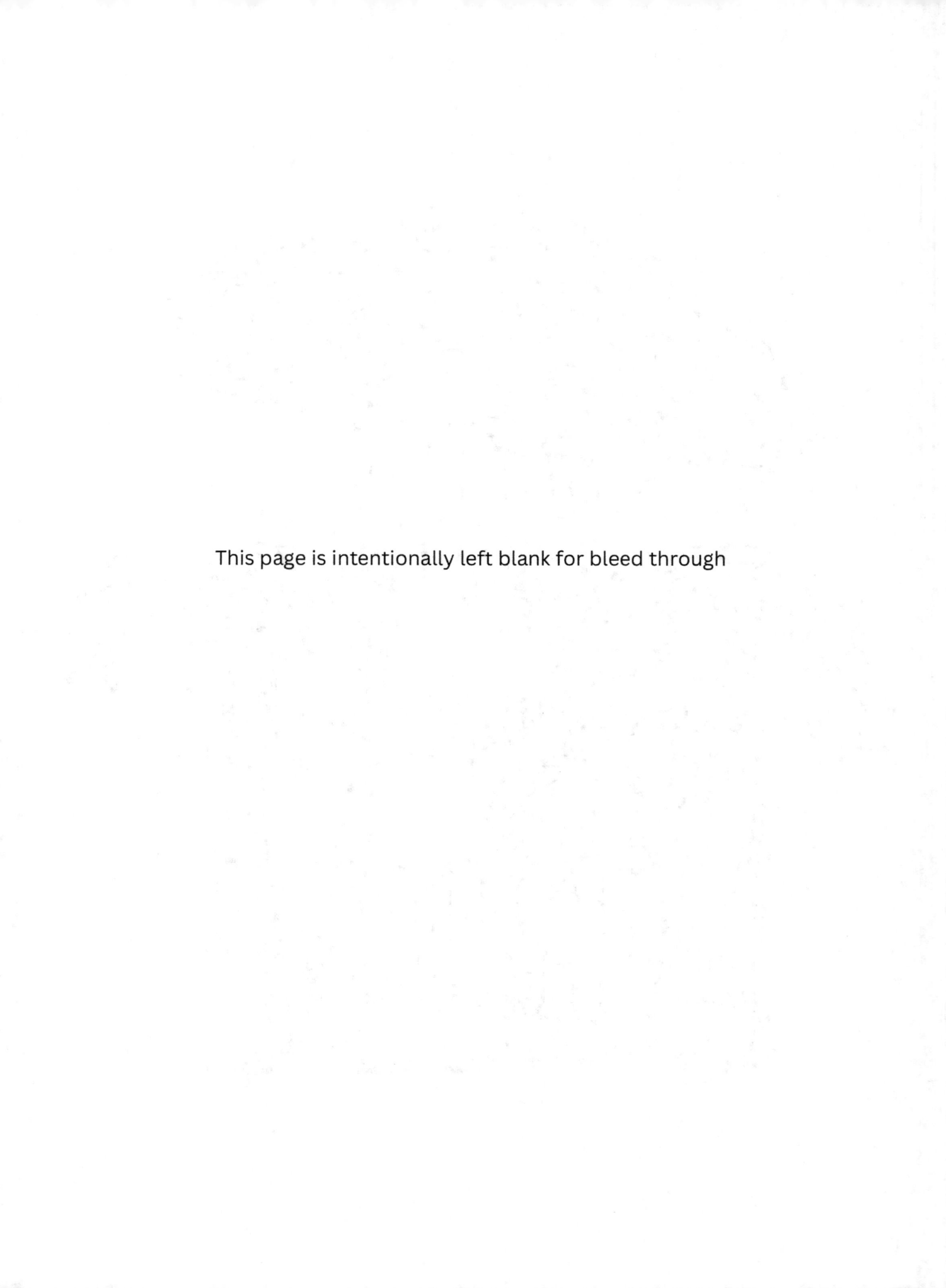

This page is intentionally left blank for bleed through

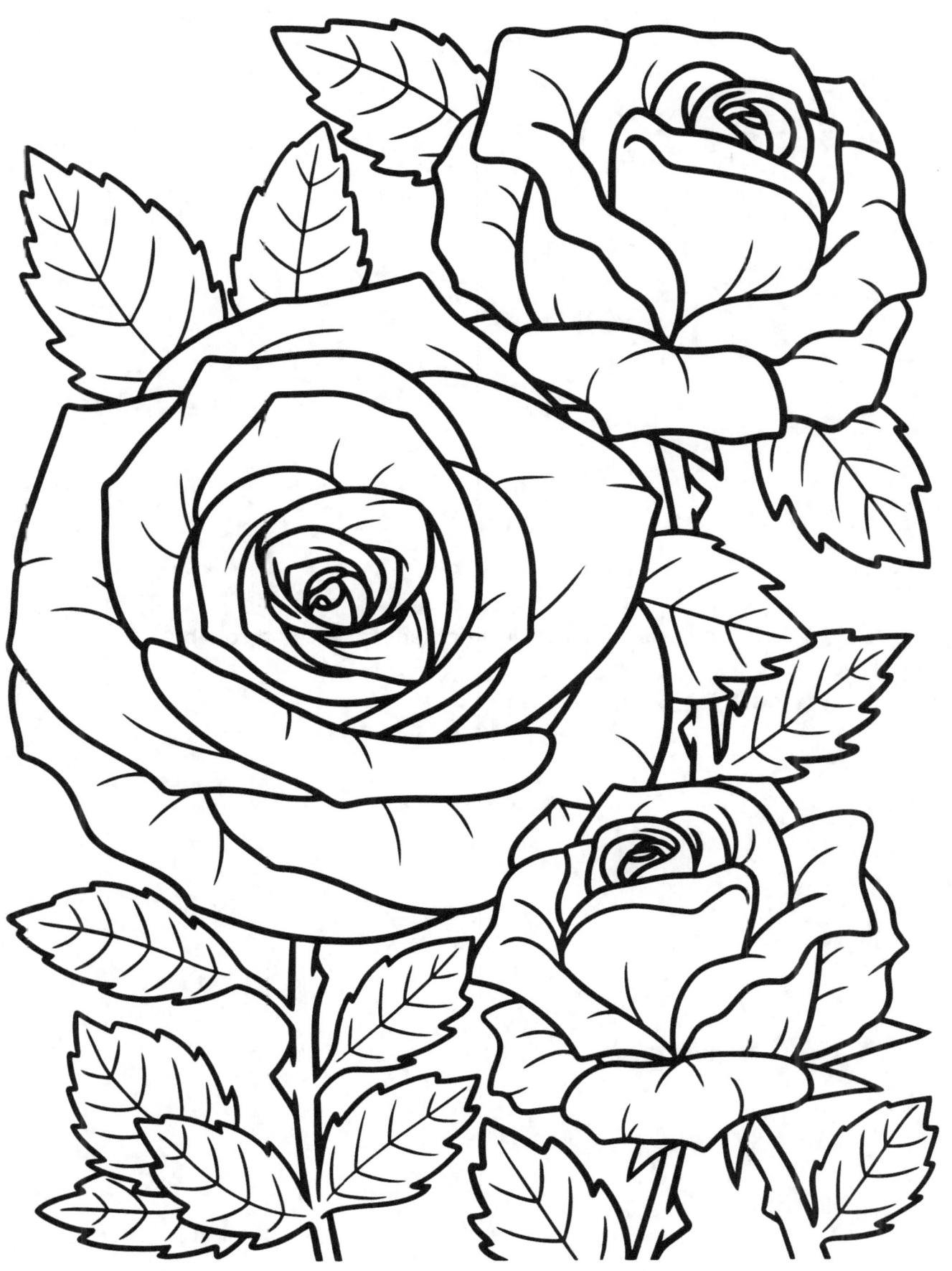

This page is intentionally left blank for bleed through

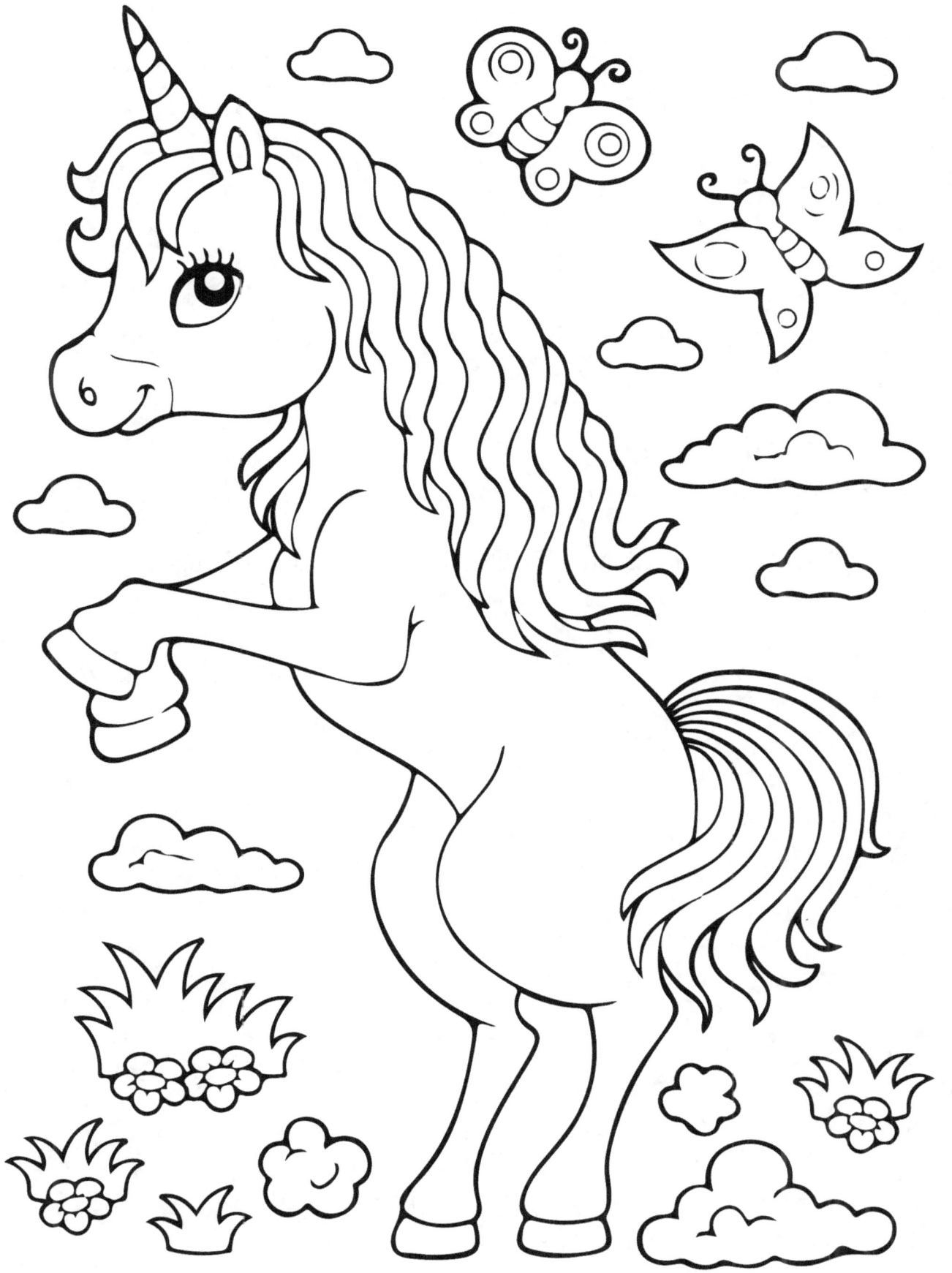

This page is intentionally left blank for bleed through

AUTHOR BIO
K. Rose - Author
www.KRoseAuthor.net
https://geni.us/KRoseNewsletter

K. Rose has been a part of the Indie Author Community for years. Getting her
start as a reader, her keen eye led to a wonderful career in Beta and ARC (Advance
Reader Copy) reading. As a joke to her fellow Beta colleagues, she created a spoofed
blurb and cover for a story and the feedback was so positive that it sparked her to run
with it.
That stoked a fire that has her racing down a multi-genre freeway with no off-ramp in sight.
K. doesn't write to "market," and she is fairly certain that her humor and
use of puns may cause an eye roll or two, but as she likes to say, "That's how I roll."
and "Jokes are always welcome!"
She has traveled the USA extensively, including Alaska, and lived in thirty-eight of the fifty
states. Home is now the beautiful state of Wisconsin, where she dreams up
her stories in the company menagerie of
furbabies, including five puppies, five rescue kitties, twenty something chickens ruled by a
rooster named Chicken Parm, six turkeys, six ducks, and a ninety-gallon tropical fish tank.
Life will always be interesting for K. Rose, which will fuel her works and keep her
muses singing, come join the chorus.

Other Works By K. Rose

The Prophecy of the Water Sprite - https://books2read.com/u/m2ROWr
Midsummer Night's Haunting - https://books2read.com/MidsummerNight
The Elven Prince - https://books2read.com/u/me9wRA
Pretty Kitties - https://books2read.com/PrettyKitties
Chrysalis Club - https://www.books2read.com/chrysalisclub
In the Pines - https://www.books2read.com/thepines
Basil - https://www.books2read.com/basil
Anthology of Strange Stories - https://www.books2read.com/anthologyofstrangestories